ANU

The raj years

Shabnam Vasisht

Published in December 2009 by emp3books,
Kiln Workshops, Pilcot Road, Crookham Village,
Fleet, Hampshire, GU51 5RY, England

©Shabnam Vasisht

The author asserts then moral right to be identified as the author of this work

ISBN-13: 978-1-907140-06-8

www.emp3books.com

ii

To my grandparents,
Purna and Kanchan,
for giving me my mother.

PREFACE

I started to write this book with the intention of recording my mother's interesting and inspiring life for family only. When her friends expressed an interest in reading it, I decided to approach it from a different angle. I have written it as a narrative, taking care to explain Indian words, places and customs for the benefit of the wider readership. The inclusion of names simply serves as a reminder to family members and need not distract the ordinary reader.

During the course of writing I noticed my mother's life was divided into four distinct sections. Packing them all into one book would have been too rambling and bulky. Producing a book to cover each section seemed to be the sensible thing to do. In this, the first part, I cover her life under the British raj. She married shortly after Independence, so I took advantage of the natural break to end this section of her memoir. The dramatic change in her life after that is a book in itself and will comprise the second part of her story.

I have relied largely on my mother's notes and memories for material. At 89 years it is hard to accurately recall one's youth, so I apologise for any discrepancies in dates or events. The photographs are not necessarily in chronological order. I dipped into my limited supply to find photos that best illustrate their chapters.

I am proud my mother lived a life that was interesting to record – I hope it will be equally interesting to read.

CONTENTS

1

PURNA AND KANCHAN

. The Kanchan Lata is a delicate white flower on a sinuous vine. Purna loved his Kanchan. She was pure and beautiful as the flower she was named after. He knew she was for him the first time he saw her.

Purna, an old boy of Scottish Kirk School, Calcutta, worked in Saharanpur, in north India. Now, he was back in Bengal to seek a wife. Dispensing with the traditional route of finding a bride, Purna confided in his vicar that he was looking for one and wanted to choose her himself.

'Come to morning service in Christ Church,' said the priest, 'there is a girl next in line for marriage in the Pandey family.'

Standing a discreet distance from the west door of the Calcutta church, Purna watched as a Bengali family swept in, the women with their heads covered in gauzy saris, the men in starched white dhotis and kurtas. They had to be the Pandeys – he was told they always sat in the second pew. He immediately recognised Kanchan, from the rector's description. After the service, he could not wait to whisper to the priest that he wished to approach the Pandey family with a proposal.

A 'viewing' was arranged with the oldest Pandey son, Dhiren, who had taken over as head of the family of twelve on the death of their father. Kanchan and her sisters had boarded in the

Diocesan Girls' School, after which Kanchan went on to train as a teacher. On the appointed day, big brother presented himself at the training college and explained the urgency of his visit. The principal summoned Kanchan to her office, ordered her to wear her best silk sari, put jasmine flowers in her braided hair and go home for the day with her brother. Having guessed the purpose of the mission, and in no mood to be viewed by a prospective husband, Kanchan rebelled in the only way she could. To her brother's horror, she presented herself in her plainest cotton sari, with her long, black hair dripping wet. Nevertheless, he hurried home with her, ranting all the way, to meet the waiting Purna. Imagining her to be shy and docile from his only glimpse of her, Purna was delighted to see the girl had spirit. There and then he asked her brother for her hand and Dhiren was happy to tick another sister off his list.

Purna sought permission to correspond with Kanchan. Her brother agreed. As a concession to modern times, he even allowed her fiancé to send her the occasional gift, so long as it was nothing more personal than a book. But occasionally, when flicking through the pages of an innocent book, Kanchan came upon a pair of fine silk stockings, a lace handkerchief or the odd penned note. Her high moral standards prevented her from replying. This was very gratifying to her future husband.

And so Kanchan Lata Pandey and Purna Chandra Sarkar were married in Christ Church, Calcutta. The bride wore a cream silk sari, embellished with gold. Her silk blouse, unlike the traditional Indian choli, was in the Victorian style – fitted and long-sleeved with pin-tucks, lace trim and tiny mother of pearl buttons down the front. The year was 1917 – the Bolsheviks were seizing power in Russia and in India, a baby girl called Indira Nehru was born, who would one day lead her country.

After the church ceremony, the two families and their friends repaired to the Pandeys' house for the marriage feast. There were the bride's six sisters, the older ones all bearing the middle name Lata, after flowering creepers. This tradition stopped after Kanchan, when a relative remarked that Latas were 'creeping all over the family'. With three girls already married, there remained two more in line after Kanchan. Of their five brothers, the youngest had died at just three weeks old when accidentally dropped from his brother Dhiren's arms. Only one brother still remained single.

On Purna's side, two of his three sisters were married, while the third returned to her Hindu roots and lived a meditative life in an ashram in Cawnpore. When Purna's mother died, his father went to live with the oldest of his three sons, Subodh, who was Chief Superintendent in the Secretariat in Calcutta. He was married, with three daughters.

The Pandeys' large villa on Allenby Road had extensive gardens and fruit trees. It was acquired by their late father when he was Audit Officer in the Secretariat. Later, most of the land was compulsorily purchased to allow for Calcutta's tram network.

For the wedding feast, the newlyweds and their guests sat cross-legged on rush floor-mats and ate off clean banana leaves. First, they had a little white fudge in the shape of a conch shell – to 'sweeten the tongue'. When guests had eaten the sondesh, the next course of luchi (puffy fried bread) and fresh vegetable dishes were placed on the leaves. After this, came rice (typically soggy in the Bengali style) with fish curry and accompanying condiments, followed by sweetened yoghurt. For dessert they had russogola – that Bengali favourite of little white dumplings in sugary syrup. No meal could conclude without paan – pungent betel leaf, folded into a tricone, containing lime and catechu pastes, spices, chopped betel nuts and tobacco. An aid to digestion, paan also served as the post-meal cigarette.

The next day the newlyweds set off for the town of Saharanpur, in the United Provinces, where Purna was Personal Assistant to a judge in the District Court. Having lived in Calcutta all her life, Kanchan was used to the hustle and bustle of a large city that had been the capital of India until 1912. Now, she was expected to adapt, not just to a new role in life but also to a small town in a completely alien part of the country. She had to learn to speak Hindi instead of her native Bengali. For the rest of her life she spoke Hindi with a strong Bengali accent.

Purna rose early to go to the market, returning with meat, fish and vegetables as well as north Indian snacks and sweets for his young bride to try. Being used to mild winters in Calcutta, Kanchan found Saharanpur much cooler, especially at night. Ever sensitive to his wife's needs, Purna had English-style flannel nightgowns tailored for her. She had never worn such garments before. She was soon to learn that life would be full of interesting and exciting new experiences with her husband. His modern ideas would prove invaluable through a future of huge political change in India.

In August 1918, Kanchan gave birth to their first child, a boy, christened Shubimol Chandra. It was mandatory to have an English name, to differentiate between Indian Christians and Hindus or Muslims, so they added Cecil to his name. To his father he was always Sunny while his mother called him Gullu, after the midwife on delivering the baby, exclaimed, 'Hai, Gulbadan!'(O, silky body). The new mother valued the advice of her neighbour, Mrs Pratt, whose husband worked in the courts with Purna. An elderly, live-in nursemaid helped Kanchan with the baby.

Two years later, Kanchan became pregnant again. Struck down with typhoid, she became gravely ill, drifting in and out of consciousness. Two attempts by the doctor to terminate the pregnancy failed. Purna intervened before the third attempt and the doctor agreed to let nature take its course. Not long after, on April 6, a baby girl was born. When Purna entered the bedroom to see the newborn, he found Sunny snuggled up beside the heavily sedated Kanchan, but no sign of the baby. The nursemaid had placed her string cot beside Kanchan's bed, ever ready to attend to her memsahib's needs. Here, Purna found his new baby daughter, so tiny he could hold her in the palm of his hand. The fight this little scrap had put up to survive in the womb filled her father with awe. She was a tiny atom (Anu) and his little princess, nay queen. And so he called her Anurani – Little Queen.

When Kanchan was strong enough, the family travelled to Calcutta where their daughter was christened in Christ Church. Her English name was Lylie and her parents always marvelled they never encountered another girl with the same name. It eventually evolved into a more familiar 'Lally' for her mother but her father always called her 'Pully' because, he said, she had pulled through despite the doctor's attempts to prevent her birth.

2
ABODE OF ALLAH

Lylie Anurani was just six weeks old when Purna was transferred to Allahabad, the capital of United Provinces. It pleased the Sarkars to find the Pratts were moving to Allahabad too, leading to a lifelong friendship.

Named Prayag in the early Hindu Scriptures, the Moghul Emperor Akbar renamed the city in 1583. He called it 'Allah-a-bad' or Abode of Allah. In 1801, the East India Company acquired it from its ruler, the Nawab of Avadh. After the first struggle for independence in 1857, power was transferred to the British Crown.

In recent years, the city had gained prominence in the campaign for freedom from British rule, initiated by the inauguration of Mahatma Gandhi's non-violent movement. Allahabad's leading family, the Nehrus, lived in two grand mansions, Anand Bhavan and Swaraj Bhavan. Their name was synonymous with India's struggle for independence, ending in a political dynasty that would give the country three future Prime Ministers.

While aware of Allahabad's position in present-day history, Purna and Kanchan did not realize the important role the city would play in the future of their own family. They teetered on the brink of a simmering movement that would eventually bubble to the surface and no one would escape the boiling froth.

Politics aside, Allahabad was most famous for being the confluence point of India's two holiest rivers, the Ganges and the Jamuna. A third underground river, Saraswati, joined them at this point, her blue ribbon dividing the muddy brown and sludgy green of the two mightier rivers. According to Hindu mythology, this site was chosen by Lord Brahma, the Creator, to become the king of all pilgrimage centres – the Tirth Raj. Apart from hosting massive holy fairs, the confluence or Sangam was a favourite picnic spot for city folk.

The Sarkars' new home, in West Khusru Bagh, consisted of rooms around a large courtyard, where the family slept on warm summer nights. The only Indians on the street, they were surrounded by British and Anglo-Indian families.

Close by, a magnificent Victorian building housed the railway station. Travellers emerging from the building were engulfed by a rush of drivers clamouring for business. Cycle-rickshaws, with brightly painted, concertinaed canopies, rang their tinkling bells. The horse-drawn 'tonga' rocked back and forth on two wheels as it hurtled through the crowded streets – its pair of seats positioned back-to-back. A couple of passengers sat beside the tonga-wallah, with an unfortunate view of the horse's behind, while others faced the oncoming traffic. And then there was the 'ekka' – another horse-drawn vehicle, peculiar to Allahabad and northern Muslim towns. Balanced high above the ekka's two big wheels, passengers huddled precariously on a little platform and held on to the bars of its canopy for dear life. Both horse-drawn vehicles afforded great fun as they 'rocked and rolled' along bumpy roads. Experienced ekka travellers even became blasé enough to let go of the bars.

A gregarious man, Purna stopped to talk to vehicle-drivers and coolies when he passed the railway station on his way to work. He became well-known in the area, acknowledging greetings of 'Salaam Sahib' as he walked to the High Court, a short distance away. He was especially impressed by a polite and genial tonga-wallah called Jagannath. The moustachioed man soon became the family's regular tonga-wallah, transporting them around Allahabad for years to come.

Jagannath, Purna and Holly before a trip in the tonga.

Even more frantic activity greeted the traveller inside the station. On long platforms, stalls served tea, ready-mixed with milk and sugar, in earthen kulhars, to be smashed after use. Jostling for position with the tea, food stalls sold hot samosas and pakoras in disposable bowls, made from leaves pinned together with twigs. Broken earthenware cups and leaf-bowls littered the railway tracks. Like all self-respecting stations, Allahabad boasted the famous mobile newsagent and bookstore, Wheelers. But the most important vendors were the paan-bidi wallahs who dispensed their wares from trays suspended from their necks. The popular paan was hastily prepared with preferred fillings and wrapped in one of the thirty-five different varieties of betel leaf. Bidis (tobacco rolled in dry leaves) and cigarettes, generally Gold Flake and Capstan, completed the seller's stock. The call of 'P-a-a-n! Bidi! Ci-ga-rrr-ate!' was a well-known cry in all northern railway stations.

Often, passengers set up camp along the platform walls, having arrived on foot or by bullock carts from neighbouring villages, to board a train from the city. Sitting and sleeping on floor mats, surrounded by tin trunks and bed-rolls, they cooked simple food on little kerosene stoves while patiently awaiting their trains.

And of course, no railway station was complete without the coolies in their distinctive red shirts with little brass licence plates tied to their upper arms. Large turbans helped them balance heavy luggage on their heads. They usually loitered in groups, smoking bidis or chewing paan, until a train came into view.

The sight of the great, black, smoke-belching dragon snaking its way into the station churned up a frenzy of motion. Vendors ran alongside the slowing train, pushing their wares through windows, off-loading as much as possible before the train moved off again. Wheelers book carts were jostled by paan-bidi wallahs, while beggars materialised from nowhere, to add to the mayhem. Summoned by travellers, railway sweepers suddenly appeared, in navy uniforms, to hastily clean toilets and brush carriage floors. Men and women, bearing earthen pots of water on their heads, rushed by the windows pouring water into tumblers, held out by thirsty passengers. For those who had the time and need to stretch their legs, several taps on the platform provided water for washing and drinking.

Weaving their way through all this, with tin trunks on their heads and bed-rolls and bags hanging from arms, were the coolies. Despite their heavy burden they ran up and down the flyovers to the appointed platform, their passengers scurrying behind them. They forced their way into carriages, shoving luggage under berths and into any available space. There then followed the inevitable haggling over price, before the coolies took their money and dashed out again for that much-needed bidi. Until the next train steamed in...

The station building housed the railway offices and waiting-rooms for the three classes of travel, with varying degrees of comfort. A large refreshment room provided sit-down meals for travellers. Allahabad, being a meal station, also supplied several hundred trays of food to trains, the order having been telegraphed from a few stations down the line. The North Indian Railway (NIR) breakfast menu consisted of toast and omelette or boiled egg, with tea. Lunch or dinner menus were limited to three choices – vegetarian, non-vegetarian and English. The first two, known as thalis, were served in stainless steel dishes. They consisted of rice, daal, chapatti and raita – the only difference being the non-vegetarian tray had a chicken or mutton curry while the other had a vegetable dish. And, of course, both meals were accompanied by the obligatory poppadums and pickles. The English meal – meat or fish cutlets and freshly fried potato chips – arrived on a china plate. And, of course, it was accompanied by the obligatory tomato ketchup. The first two menus reflected regional changes, depending on the route of the train. The English menu, however, remained unchanged throughout the country.

Upon the arrival of a train, railway bearers emerged from the kitchens in white hand-woven shirts and trousers. Their turbans bore striped bands in the colours of the railway, with the letters NIR or other, depending on the Railway Division. Bearers ran along the platform, deftly balancing stacks of trays, to be delivered to assigned carriages in the hour that the train halted at the meal station. For trains that boasted dining cars, there was no such panic. Travellers could dine at leisure while taking a break from their own carriage between stations.

The 'Dead Letter Office' was merely a notice-board, entitled 'DLO', situated outside the Station Master's office. Allahabad's undeliverable letters were pinned to the board and secured behind a chicken-wire door. The idea was that local folk could search the board for mail with their names and request the Station Master for their letter.

While these scenes were typical of all railway stations, Allahabad, being a junction, had twice the excitement.

3
COURT CIRCULARS

Purna was proud to be working in the Allahabad High Court. Originally located in Agra, the court moved to its present location in 1869, as 'The High Court of Judicature at Allahabad'. Designed by Frank Lishman in a blend of eastern and western styles, its domed centre was flanked by long arcades with engrailed arches. One of the first High Courts in India, declared open in 1916 by Viceroy Lord Chelmsford, it boasted the largest Chief Justice's courtroom of all High Courts in the country.

Its unusual double-roof, topped by Allahabad tiles, was designed to combat the summer heat. When Sunny was seven and Anu five, Purna decided they were old enough to appreciate the unique 'air-conditioning' of the court room. He seated them in the public gallery and asked them to be quiet until he was finished. Unfortunately, Sunny discovered a paper pin and, bored by legal arguments, fell prey to a brotherly temptation. He pricked Anu's arm with the pin. The flurry and squeals from the public gallery did not escape the judge. He ordered the immediate removal of the offenders and the two children were unceremoniously hustled out by the peon. They sat on a bench outside in the scorching heat, till Purna was ready to take them home – so much for an afternoon in their father's 'air-conditioned office'.

As Personal Assistant to various judges, Purna often travelled with the court to cases in towns with no High Court. In the warmer months, the courts and the government moved to the cool hill-station of Simla, the 'summer capital' of India. At almost 7,000 feet high, the town clung to the slopes of the Himalayan foothills, overlooking a spectacular valley. The main street, The Mall, ran along a ridge and was the fashionable centre of town from which all vehicles were banned and, until WW1, all 'natives', except rickshaw-pullers and Indian royalty. The Mall was lined by English-style buildings, the most famous being the Gaiety Theatre. Summer balls, picnics and bridge-parties were legendary. For those British women whose husbands could not escape the plains, Simla offered many opportunities for secret dalliances. A favourite rendezvous point, christened 'Scandal Corner' by Rudyard Kipling, survives to this day.

Purna saved his generous daily allowance to buy a trunkful of colourful saris and woollen shawls for his beloved wife. She complained that he brought back very little for the children. So off he would go to the local market to buy them toys.

For Purna, his wife always came first. The couple was invited to a garden party when Purna was Personal Assistant to Chief Justice, Sir John Thom. At the party, Kanchan admired Lady Thom's champagne coloured court shoes and raved about them long after they got home. The next day, Purna took her to the best shoe-maker in town, a Chinaman called Fookson. Yes, Mr Fookson had indeed hand-made Lady Thom's shoes. Purna ordered an exact copy for Kanchan. Her feet were measured and a few days later she received a smart wooden box. Inside, nestling in folds of pink tissue, were her shoes. Mr Fookson supplied the family's shoes for the next three generations. Decades later, when her grandchildren admired a large portrait of Kanchan over the fireplace, their attention was always drawn to her champagne 'Lady Thom' shoes.

On his return from trips, Purna regaled Kanchan with tales of his experiences. Like the time in Agra when he was put up in the home of an Italian barrister, Mr Regalini. That night in bed, Purna felt a cold touch. Nervously opening his eyes, he glimpsed a pale female hand with a wedding ring, before a young woman disappeared through the door. Next morning the servants anxiously hovered round him at breakfast until finally, one of them asked if he had slept well. When told about the vision, they said she was their master's dead daughter. It seemed they were aware she appeared in 'her' room and hoped their guest could verify it.

There were funny stories, too. After a gruelling day at the local court, the legal team relaxed on the verandah of the guest house, sipping their Tom Collins' and nimbu panis (fresh lemon drink). The tranquil mood was shattered by a Bengali member of the party stumbling out of the house, hastily pulling on his trousers and shouting, 'My Lord! Phosh!' The man had come upon a cobra in the toilet and, in his panic, couldn't remember the English word for snake. After that his colleagues referred to him as 'My Lord Phosh'.

Kanchan in her 'Lady Thom Shoes'

Tragedy touched the courts when a legal party went on a shooting expedition and Justice Dillon shot a tiger. The animal fell to the ground and as the party cautiously approached it, the wounded tiger sprang up and mauled the judge to death. The next day the courts remained closed in memory of the judge.

One morning, Purna recounted a strange dream to Kanchan. He was in a train and as it pulled into a station, panic-stricken people were running up and down the platform shouting, 'Go back! Go back!' Kanchan believed this to be a premonition.

Shortly after, the court boarded a train but part-way through the journey it seemed unable to get a signal for the station ahead. After a while, the conductor went through the carriages, warning passengers of a cholera epidemic in the next town. The train could go no further. The conductor advised passengers to return home or take a different route. The legal party returned to Allahabad, deferring cases until the town was declared safe again.

In his study at home, Purna typed up the reports he took in court, in his own peculiar short-hand, and Kanchan proof-read them. When Anu was old enough, she took on the job of proof-reader from her mother.

While Purna was away with the court, Kanchan ran the household with a small staff of cook, ayah and gardener. Her neighbour, an Englishwoman called Mrs Povey, taught her feminine skills – dress-making, knitting, embroidery and crochet. Kanchan delighted in producing original clothes for Sunny and Anu. She was loath to cut Sunny's beautiful curls and people often wondered if he was a boy or girl. Sunny's standard reply was, 'When my hair is long, I'm a girl, when it's cut, I'm a boy.'

When the children were in bed and the servants dismissed, Kanchan, an avid reader, turned to books to fill the lonely nights. She devoured novels like 'The Mighty Atom' and 'The Soul of Lilith' by her favourite author, Marie Corelli. Years later, along with fairy tales of Bengal, she narrated Marie Corelli novels to her grandchildren at bedtime. They heard one chapter a night and could not wait for bedtime to get the next instalment.

4
ATUL CHANDRA SARKAR

One Sunday, while playing in the garden, Anu saw a railway coolie in a red uniform, with a trunk on his head, struggling to open the gate. He was followed by a tall, elderly gentleman in silk kurta and white dhoti. Anu ran indoors to tell her mother. Kanchan emerged from the house, quickly covered her head with her sari and folded her hands in namaste. Purna, following the sound of voices at the gate, was surprised to see his father, in a deeply distressed state. The coolie explained that the old man had emerged from Allahabad station, confused and disorientated. When confronted by the clamour of vehicle-drivers he asked if anyone knew where Mr. P.C. Sarkar lived. This particular coolie knew 'Sarkar Sahib' and offered to take him the short distance to his son's house. Purna thanked and paid the coolie, tipping him generously. He took his father's little trunk while Kanchan led her agitated father-in-law into the house.

After they calmed him down, he told them of the appalling treatment he had endured at the hands of his eldest son in Calcutta. Mean of spirit and conservative in outlook, Subodh did not believe in educating his daughters. As they reached puberty he set about arranging their marriages. His three daughters married three brothers, all farmers. Having rid himself of the girls, he became increasingly resentful at having to look after his father. Although the old man handed his pension over to them each month, Subodh and his wife stinted him food and other necessities. After months of suffering, he protested.

'You don't have to live here if you don't like it,' screeched his daughter-in-law, 'you have other children. Go live with them!'

Subodh was silent. The old man realized that his son agreed with his wife. They wanted rid of him. Packing a few meagre belongings in a little trunk, he boarded the train to Allahabad, with no time to wire his arrival.

From that day on, Atul Chandra Sarkar made his home with his second son, Purna, where his daughter-in-law looked after him with respect and devotion. She was glad to have a father figure again, remembering how her own father had lost his sight minutes before he died.

'Why have you snuffed out the lamp, Gyano?' were his last words to his wife.

'Dadu' (grandfather) to his grandchildren, Atul delighted in Sunny and Anu. Every afternoon, when snack hawkers passed the gate, he opened his little trunk and withdrew one anna each for the children. From Babu Lal they bought paper thin puri – deep-fried chapatti – with a dollop of halwa or bright pink candy floss called 'old woman's hair'. Apart from this, Atul's trunk was never opened. Since his arrival, all his clothes were new.

Each morning the barber arrived with the tools of his trade in a clapped-out Gladstone bag. After expertly shaving Atul with his

Sweeny Todd blade, he rounded off the treatment with a champi – head massage. When necessary, he trimmed his hair and moustache and de-waxed his ears with little copper spoons. While he worked away he brought gossip from the bazaar. Years later, when Purna retired, he continued the tradition of having the barber call each morning.

When Anu was not quite two, another baby girl was born into the family. She was delivered at home, just as the new day was breaking, so they named her Aruna, meaning Dawn. It also reflected the name of Kanchan's sister, Arulata, who had died in childbirth. Anu immediately decided she had a live doll to play with so they added Dolly to her name.

One evening, the milkman stopped by the house to tell Purna that his father was lying by the roadside. Atul had left the house for his daily stroll round the area. Purna and a neighbour rushed to the scene and carried the old man home. Dr Roy informed the family that Atul had suffered a stroke. Purna employed a man-servant to attend to his personal needs while Kanchan nursed her father-in-law with loving care. He suffered a further series of mild strokes and, although incapacitated at first, eventually managed to recover. After his fifth stroke, he lost his speech and only Kanchan could understand his grunts and growls. One day, she came running out to the courtyard as the old man's growls got louder. He was drawing her attention to Anu. The toddler had dipped a palm hand-fan in a bucket of water and was merrily fanning herself in the cold winter air. A smack on her little wet bottom soon put an end to that. Eventually Atul regained his speech enough to be clearly understood.

On a hot summer's day in June 1924, when Kanchan was heavily pregnant again, Atul had his sixth stroke. This time it looked like it would be his last. Relatives, summoned from Calcutta, filled the courtyard where he lay. Subodh, fearing the contempt of his siblings, stayed away. Dr Roy and the English Civil Surgeon of Allahabad kept vigil with the family by the old man's bed. Oil lamps lit the courtyard all night long. His death rattle resounded through the house.

Around midnight, the trauma of it all caused Kanchan to go into labour. Dr Christie arrived as fast as she could and as one life was ebbing away, another entered the world. As soon as the new baby's shrill cry reached the courtyard, Atul was jolted into consciousness again. He raised his head and asked to see the baby. Unwashed and wrapped in a clean towel, the infant was placed in her Dadu's arms. In a strong voice he blessed her, calling on God to shower the new baby with wealth and good fortune. The doctors were amazed. Atul's 'miracle' return from the tunnel of death was recorded by the Civil Surgeon in Allahabad's Medical Journal. The baby was named Purnima, the feminine version of her father's name, meaning Full Moon. They chose her English name, Molly, to rhyme with the sister before her. As an adult, her life was of such enormous wealth and luxury that her siblings always credited this good fortune

23

to the unique circumstances of their Dadu's blessing.

Atul went on to live for another four years, long enough to see the birth of his fourth granddaughter. The new baby was so adored by her older sisters that they named her Priti Rani – Queen of Love.

On Priti's first birthday, Atul suffered his last and fatal stroke. He was 89. In the search for funeral instructions, Purna opened his father's little trunk. He found the old man's funeral clothes neatly laid out in it – new white dhoti edged in gold, white muslin kurta and stole. They were the only clothes he had packed when he left his eldest son's home so hurriedly. Also in the trunk was the bag of anna and paisa pieces for his grandchildren's daily candy floss.

Atul was buried in Allahabad cemetery and the two plots beside him endowed for Purna and Kanchan. Later, a tombstone was erected and a heavy iron chain placed around the grave. An annual fee was paid to the authorities to tend the grave.

Anu was bereft. The children had been sent to a friend's house so she never saw her grandfather laid out in his coffin. For days she wandered through the house, calling, 'Dadu!' expecting to find him in one of the rooms. Her mother told her he had 'gone to heaven' but Anu could not believe he had left without telling her.

5

TIFFIN TIME

When Sunny was five and Anu, four, they enrolled in the nursery section of St Anne's High School, catering mostly to Indian Christian and Anglo-Indian girls.

The best 'English medium' schools at the time were run by Protestant and Roman Catholic churches. They followed the Anglo-Indian Education System, devised by Cambridge. (Until the end of the 1960s the school-leaving exam was called the 'Senior Cambridge Exam'. Papers were shipped to England for marking, the results returned to India three months later.)

At 5.30 each morning, with two little children clutching at her sari, Kanchan waited at the gate. In the dim haze of dawn a swinging lantern became barely visible, accompanied by a creaking sound. Eventually a bullock-cart appeared and Sunny and Anu clambered onto it. Off they went to school, picking up other children along the way, among them Sunny's best friend, Kenny David. The ayah, hired by the families to mind the children, would fall asleep as would the cart-driver. The bullock knew his way and slowed down at regular stops to pick up his little passengers. While their minders dozed, the boys jumped off the cart and raced it all the way to school. As they passed tamarind trees, they stopped to collect the acid beans that set their teeth on edge. They jumped on again when the bullock cart arrived at its destination at 7 a.m., just as the schoolbell was ringing.

On their first day back Anu claimed she had learned English at school.

'What did the teacher say?' asked her father.

'Yes', replied Anu.

'And what did you say?' he continued.

'Yes', said Anu.

And so it went on, with 'Yes' being the answer to every question. She had learned her first English word. Purna remarked to Kanchan that it was a clear sign their daughter would have a positive attitude to life.

Each morning the cook packed tiffins for the two children to snack during their break. They sat in groups under shady trees and ate cold omelette and chapatti. One day, Anu, intrigued by the small group of children who queued for tiffins doled out by the nuns, joined them. She tried to share her warm lamb cutlets and chips with her red-faced brother. He refused, instead reporting the incident to their father. Purna explained to Anu that the food was for girls who boarded in the school. She should stick to her own tiffin. A few weeks later she joined another queue and was delighted to receive a pretty pink frock. When she brought it home her father told her the clothes were for children who had no parents to buy for them. He asked Anu to return it to the nun with thanks. Too embarrassed to do so she tried to persuade Sunny to return it for her, to no avail.

Anu and Sunny

With head bowed Anu approached the 'clothes' nun. Her apology and frock accepted, she skipped happily back to the classroom.

Sunny had his own problems. Trusting him to pay the school bill, Purna placed money in an envelope and asked Sunny to give it to his teacher. In the rough and tumble of boisterous games, the wad fell out his pocket and Sunny had to face his father's wrath when he got home. Luckily, an honest playground sweeper found the sealed envelope and handed it into the office. Purna rarely placed Sunny in a position of responsibility again.

When Priti was eighteen months old, she contracted bronchitis. On Christmas Day 1928, Kanchan decided to stay with her while Purna took the other children to church. On their return they found Kanchan still holding and gently rocking the toddler, unaware that her baby's breathing had ceased. It took a day and night of gentle persuasion before Kanchan surrendered her baby for burial. Priti Rani was interred close to her Dadu in Allahabad cemetery.

A year later, on New Year's Eve, Kanchan, carrying her sixth child, went into labour. Sunny ran all the way to his friend Kenny David's house and alerted his mother. Dr David returned with Sunny and, in the early hours of New Year's Day 1930, she delivered a baby girl.

The infant was christened Smriti – Remembrance, in memory of the sister before her. The festive season presented the perfect name to follow her older sisters – Holly. Her mother, though, always called her 'Baby'.

Sunny was addressed as 'Dada' by his sisters while all the younger girls called Anu, 'Didi' – the respectful terms, in Bengal, for older siblings. The address often suffixed a name to differentiate between various dadas and didis. Strictly speaking it should have been Anu didi, or the more familiar Anudi, to the three younger sisters, Dollydi to the two younger ones and finally Mollydi to Holly. But after Anu the didis fell by the wayside.

6
WEST KHUSRU BAGH

The family's house took its address from the adjoining Khusru Bagh – a trio of Moghul monuments, built in 1622. The Islamic-style gardens served as a park for local people, mostly in the dewy, pink softness of dawn or the balmy stillness of summer nights. In the evenings the gardens filled with ayahs and their charges, out to enjoy the fresh air. The children clambered on the monument to Prince Khusru – murdered by his brother, Shah Jehan (of Taj Mahal fame), for being named successor by their father, Emperor Jehangir. They played hide-and-seek between the pillars of his sister Princess Nissar's mausoleum. Their favourite building was that of Shah Begum, Jehangir's first wife. The Rajput (Hindu) queen was said to have poisoned herself in despair at the animosity between the Emperor and his son. Her two-storeyed mausoleum offered lots of places to hide and heights from which to jump. One evening, the family's ayah chatted with other minders while the children scrambled on the tombs. A piercing scream alerted her to Anu, lying at the bottom of Shah Begum's monument. The ayah hailed a tonga to take them all home, Anu's limp and painful arm causing her to bawl all the way. Purna immediately fired the ayah, who added her wails to the child's, begging Kanchan to intervene. Leaving his wife to reassure the ayah, Purna took Anu to the Railway Hospital.

Her arm was put in splints and bandaged to the tips of her fingers. In the morning when Kanchan saw Anu's middle finger peeping out, she admitted to Purna that she had fretted and prayed all night that her child's arm had not been amputated.

'Why didn't you just ask me, instead of tormenting yourself?' he rebuked.

'If you had said she had lost her arm', replied Kanchan,' I would not have had the chance to ask God to save it.'

The house in West Khusru Bagh was off the Grand Trunk Road, an ancient trade-route. Originally called The Long Walk, it stretched from Afghanistan to the east coast of India, passing many major cities on its way. On the morning of the Shi'ite festival of Moharrum, little green tents sprang up all along the Grand Trunk Road. The Muslim festival commemorated the martyrdom of Prophet Mohammed's grandsons, Hasan and Hussain, on the battlefield of Karbala, on the banks of the Euphrates. Anu and her siblings watched from their courtyard as men and children lined the road, while the green tents offered purdah to the veiled Muslim women. After breakfast, the ayah hustled the Sarkar children out quickly to find a vantage viewing point for the procession. First came the Alam (standard) followed by drummers, their furious sticks beating up a thunderous clamour. Behind them came the mourners. Men with flailing swords and poles, cried out loudly, beating their chests and flagellating themselves with iron chains and leather whips in a ritual of mourning. Many, in a trance, with

31

skewers through tongues and bodies, staggered and reeled along the way.

Last of all came the tazias – replicas of the martyrs' tombs. Made from wood, paper, tinsel and fabric, they supported a whole industry of tazia-making, leading up to Moharrum. The tazia parade was interspersed, at regular intervals, by elephants. On their howdahs sat men with enormous copper pots of biryani, kebabs and rumali rotis – handkerchief-thin chapattis. Donated by wealthy Muslims, the food was doled out to the poor along the procession's route. People ran alongside the elephants, reaching out to catch flying rotis and holding up dishes for ladles of biryani. This slowed the parade down and gave the Sarkar children sufficient time to run home, gobble their lunch and dash back in time for the grand finale – the Bara (big) Tazia. As the coffin-like tazia containing effigies of the martyrs passed, women keened and howled from within their green tents. The procession wound its way to the river for the immersion of the tazias. By 4 pm it was all over and the little green tents along the route had disappeared. Flimsy tazias in gaudy pinks, greens and reds floated down the river, their slowly unravelling tinsel glinting in the light of the setting sun.

On full-moon nights, Purna hired an ekka – a rubber-tyred one, for speed. The family squashed onto the high seating platform and the horse trotted off, slowly at first as it manoeuvred its way out to the Grand Trunk Road. Once on the wide deserted highway, the ekka-wallah lashed the horse and away it galloped, its passengers laughing and singing all the way. The silver light of the moon, the cooling breeze whipped up by the speed and the thrill of managing to stay on the vehicle were the simple pleasures of the night.

The family lived in the house for a few years before it was declared dangerous, due to the negligence of the landlord. Several plots, around a field, became available in the nearby locality of Lukergunj. Word spread through the grapevine and mostly Bengali buyers snapped up the land. Purna acquired a corner site at the edge of the field. Things were looking up for the family – first a new baby and soon a new home.

Building was spread over three years. Although Purna commuted his pension to pay for the construction, he also borrowed money from the bank, in instalments. The ground-breaking ceremony took place on Easter Sunday. The parish priest placed seven metals – gold, silver, copper, lead, tin, brass and zinc, each representing a member of the family – in a stone jar and set it in a corner of the foundations. Then he laid seven bricks in a right angle formation and blessed them. Upon these seven bricks the house was built – the cornerstone, so to speak. The vicar led the family in the recitation of Psalm 127:

'Except the Lord build the house, they labour in vain that build it: except the lord keep the city, the watchman waketh but in vain....'

Construction began in earnest. Scrawny, leather-skinned men toiled to build while women carried various materials on their heads, from the delivery site to the builders. To and fro they went all day in the blazing heat, stopping only to, perhaps, feed a baby lying under the shade of a tree. They lunched on chapatti made from coarse ground wheat, daal, and wild spinach, picked from the building site. When the hot and dusty 'loo' wind blew, they carried a white onion on their person to stave off heat stroke.

Each week, freshly baked bricks were delivered from the kiln and sand, still damp, from river beds. It was sieved through a large wire mesh frame, propped at an angle, weeding out pebbles and tiny shells. Beside a white mountain of lime, a temporary tank stored water. Scaffolding was constructed from bamboo and wood, precariously held together by fraying rope and rusty nails.

The ayah often brought the children to watch. The older ones went looking for shells in the sand while Holly trailed around with her as she chatted to the women labourers. One day, the toddler broke away in search of her sisters and stumbled into the mound of lime. At her first scream, a quick-thinking labourer picked her up and dunked her in the water tank. His presence of mind saved Holly's eyes from being blinded by the lime. But for the rest of her life, she suffered from spasmodic blinking, especially when tired or excited.

7
A MAN OF LETTERS

When Anu was ten years old she took to writing to her father when he was away with the courts. In June 1930 he wrote her several letters as he was away for over a month. While Sunny and Dolly soon lost interest in letter-writing, Anu persevered. Her father was not surprised.

His letter from 'Portland House', Dalhousie, began with 'My loving little Pully, Your sweet letter to hand. So everybody dropped off except you, eh? I knew that.' Referring to Anu's complaint that Sunny had been fighting with other boys in the neighbourhood, he wrote, 'Tell Sunny to be careful or he will hear from me.'

He went on to talk about Mr Staines – his ex-brother-in-law. Purna's sister, Shiu, was Staff Nurse at a Calcutta hospital where she met an English patient, Mr Staines. After a brief courtship, she married him. The marriage was not a success. On a visit to Allahabad with his wife, Staines decided it was a good place to live. Leaving his wife to return to Calcutta alone, he took up residence in a dilapidated little house near Khusru Bagh. At his sister's request, Purna started divorce proceedings in Allahabad and the marriage came to an end. However, Purna kept up his friendship with the Englishman.

Anu wrote to her father of Mr Staines' poor health and her father replied, 'I am awfully cut up to hear about Mr Staines. Look after him as much as you can and keep him alive until I come back. I miss the old man very much and wish God will let me see him again. Remember me to him and give him my kindest regards.'

At her daughter's insistence, Kanchan bought Anu a pack of fancy writing paper and envelopes. She excitedly wrote to her father, still in Dalhousie. He replied immediately, typing the opening lines.

'My dear Pully Baba,

'You gave me quite a shock and it took me at least ten minutes to make up my mind to open your letter. It reminded me of my young days when I used to receive letters in such fashionable envelopes that I wondered who the writer was.'

He told her to ask her mother about his work in Dalhousie, as he wrote to Kanchan every week, before continuing, 'This evening I went for a walk – the scenery around here is very enchanting. There is a girls' and boys' boarding school near our house and I can hear the girls singing and playing every evening.'

Halfway through the letter Purna reverted to his small, neat handwriting to continue, 'Tell Mr Staines that I will come back soon to give him a game of chess. He must be very lonely and I pity him very much.'

Purna Chandra Sarkar

He ended with, 'I went to the bazaar this evening to see if I could buy anything suitable for you but there is nothing which I cannot get for you in Allahabad.

'With love and kisses,

'Your loving Daddy.'

In her next letter Anu reported that Sunny was behaving himself. Once more, her father replied in a part typed, part hand-written letter, 'I am very glad to know about Sunny's improvement.' He referred to Mr Staines and their game of chess again. This amused Kanchan as Purna taught her to play chess and enjoyed beating her every time... until the day *she* beat him. After that he didn't seem interested in playing with her any more.

Purna signed off with, 'I am quite well and will be going to Patiala and then to Simla and then back to home sweet home.'

From Dalhousie, Purna accompanied the court to Patiala, in the Punjab, on an extremely sensitive and high-profile case. The Maharaja of Patiala had seduced the wife of one of his subjects and was sued by the aggrieved husband. After hearing the case in Patiala the court went on to Simla.

Purna wrote to Anu from 'Rockwood', Simla, 'I have just finished all my work and am hastening to write to you lest I may not find time tomorrow. I arrived here at 2 pm yesterday after a tedious journey by motor of 125 miles. It is a very fine drive in the plains but when you begin to tackle the hills it is a round and zig-zag drive that makes you sick. I had a walk round Simla this morning and had a look at the Viceroy's house. From a distance you can see the big and imposing building but when you go near it you can't see anything as it is hidden by trees and the hills around it. From my place you can see the whole of Simla. In front of my house there is a big 'khud' or depression and then the hill rises up higher than the hill on which my house is but more houses are built on that hill. At night it is a grand sight when all the electric lights are lit like big stars.'

After enquiring about Molly's birthday party, for which he had sent money, he asked of his 'Doll Booby', 'Why doesn't she write to me?'

His attention returned to Anu at the end of the letter, 'I will try and see if I can get something nice for you from here. If not, I will get you some nice toys from Allahabad.'

Purna's letters were written on postcards with King George V stamps, costing ½ anna. At the top of the card was a small Lion and Unicorn crest with INDIA printed above it. Anu treasured these letters all her life, saving them in a yellowing envelope entitled 'My father's letters'.

Purna returned to Allahabad in July. It was a busy time as the court prepared its judgement on the various cases heard in Dalhousie, Patiala and Simla. In the case of the Maharaja of Patiala, a decision was made in favour of the commoner. Before it could be published, the victorious man's family appeared to know the outcome and commenced their celebrations. They lit up their house and garden with fairy lights and invited folk to rejoice with them at the impending humiliation of the Maharaja. The Allahabad High Court was nonplussed. An investigation was launched and a mole uncovered – My Lord Phosh. The man, who had caused such hilarity by fleeing a snake, with his trousers round his knees, was arrested. While out on bail, he had a stroke that rendered him unfit for trial. A short while later, he passed away, never having surrendered the bribe he received for revealing the judgment against the Maharaja of Patiala.

8
KANCHAN VILLA

The Sarkars' new house was finally completed in 1931. It was big, impressive, and best of all, electrified.

An arched front verandah led to the large drawing room, behind which lay the dining room. In the centre of the drawing room floor was a five-pointed star, one point for each of the five children. Both rooms were flanked by identical wings – two bedrooms on either side of the verandah; behind them, parallel with the drawing room, two larger bedrooms that opened out onto long side verandahs. The rooms flanking the dining room served as spacious dressing-rooms. Leading off from these rooms were two toilets. Commodes lined the walls and a small area with a tap was sectioned off for washing.

The kitchen was situated behind the house, a few yards from the dining room. This was the traditional way Indian houses were laid out to prevent contamination of food. The kitchen building contained the cooking room, with a row of clay chulhas, built to knee level. Food was cooked squatting in front of the coal-fired chulhas. Attached to the kitchen, the pantry held tall canisters of rice, lentils and wheat flour. Big jars of spices, sugar and tea lined the shelves. Dry goods, such as these, were usually purchased on a monthly basis. Fresh meat, fish, fruit and vegetables were bought daily, either from the market or from vendors who came to the door.

A dooli or little press, with chicken-wire doors, kept milk and other perishable foods fresh. It was left outdoors at night to keep cool.

The two rooms behind the pantry housed the only live-in domestics – cook and ayah. Their toilet was built into the boundary wall behind the kitchen.

To the left of the kitchen, the bathing house was a room used specifically for personal hygiene. In one corner a concrete tank, with three foot high walls, served as a reservoir in case of water shortage. Along another wall two taps, about four feet off the ground, allowed one to crouch under them and bathe in the running water. Buckets, basins and jugs as well as free-standing wooden towel rails furnished the room. Soaps, toothpastes, brushes, shaving mugs and other toiletries balanced on the ledge of the water-tank. A fat glass jar held ritha – black marble-like seeds that, when boiled, released herbal froth used to shampoo hair.

Along the back wall of the house, to the right, a flight of steep steps led to the roof. Room ceilings were higher than those of the verandahs, so the roof was split level. Several years after the family moved into the house, Purna built a second storey. Four steps led to two large rooms and small verandah on the higher level of the roof. No parapets protected the lower level, making it dangerous to venture too close to the edge when picking fruit off the surrounding trees.

The exterior of the house was painted a pale shade of ochre while light aqua tinted the verandah walls. The blue, glowing through the arches, gave the house a picture postcard look. The interior walls were white-washed and refreshed once a year.

Directly above the front verandah, along the edge of the roof, a concrete scroll proudly proclaimed 'KANCHAN VILLA'.

A low boundary wall ran all around the property. It was built with the fashionable bricks of the day, in the shape of a four-petalled flower. When put together, they created a lattice effect. Shrubs flanked the wide, wrought-iron front gate. A marble plaque, embedded in the left gate post, bore the engraving 'P.C. SARKAR'.

Kanchan Villa was furnished with a pleasant mix of heavy Victorian and light Indian furniture. Sofas, armchairs and teapoys furnished the drawing room. Mohras – little wicker stools, with woven coir rope seats – afforded extra seating. Purna took Kanchan to the smart shops in Civil Lines from where she bought yards and yards of tangerine Nottingham lace for drawing room curtains. Above the fireplace hung the celebrated portrait of Kanchan in her 'Lady Thom shoes'.

A grand oval table dominated the dining room. On the wall was a plaque that read:

> *Christ is the head of this house,*
> *The unseen guest at every meal,*
> *A silent listener to every conversation.*

On the wall above Purna and Kanchan's spacious double bed were two framed pictures of Jesus and the Virgin Mary. The tall mahogany wardrobes had chunky crystal handles, while the bevelled mirrors of the dressing tables were supported by little drawers for individual beauty products. The dressing rooms had built-in shelves as well as free-standing clotheshorses.

Before the excited family moved into Kanchan Villa, they held a service of blessing in their new house. A small group of friends joined them as the vicar led them in prayer.

They all joined in singing a hymn of thanksgiving:

'Now thank we all our God,
With hearts and minds and voices
Who wondrous things hath done,
In whom his world rejoices…'

The next day the family loaded its possessions on several bullock carts and happily moved into Kanchan Villa.

9
A FRUITFUL LIFE

A great deal of planning went into the layout of Kanchan Villa's garden. The forecourt was dominated by the chabutra – a circular concrete platform, approximately 18" high 10' in diameter. It displayed pots of seasonal flowers – gold, bronze and white chrysanthemums in the winter; pink, purple and red zinnias in the summer. A wide path ran around the chabutra and on either side of it, two jasmine arches led to gardens on right and left. Another path hugged the house all the way round, separating it from the garden.

Purna divided the larger left-hand plot into sections for lawn, flowers and vegetables. Low hedges of henna and bela – a scented white flower used in garlands for the hair – separated the sections.

Fruit trees took up much of the land around the house: mango, banana, guava, papaya, jack fruit, tiny lychee-like ice fruit, purple jamun plums , custard apple, lemon and lime. No garden was complete without the neem tree, valued for its antiseptic and medicinal properties. In the shade of the larger trees, smaller shrubs battled for survival: kundru – tomato-like and beloved of parrots; ber – wild, olive-sized fruit; phalsa – big, purple berry. An elegant Chinese orange tree hugged the left arch of the verandah, its top leaves stroking the 'Kanchan Villa' scroll.

The family used many of these trees and shrubs as a first-aid kit. A piece of cool, moist banana bark against the skin relieved burns. An infusion of Lemon Grass was the panacea for all respiratory tract ailments. Kanchan planted a lush specimen outside the kitchen. Licking a dollop of molasses off a mango leaf dispelled summer hives and hay fever. Milky sap from the fig tree dislodged a thorn from the flesh.

Their beauty secrets, too, were contained in the garden. Chewing on neem twigs cleansed teeth and freshened breath. The hibiscus flower, crushed and used as conditioner, resulted in healthy and glossy hair. The same flower, rubbed on leather gave it a beautiful shine, hence its alternative name, Shoe Flower. The soft, yellow pulp of the papaya applied as an enzyme-rich face-pack, cleansed and softened the skin. And the perfect substitute for perfume? A fragrant garland of roses, jasmine or bela, in the hair.

Mango trees shaded the lawn that ran along the left side of the house. The family slept under these trees on stifling summer nights. Behind the house stood two jackfruit trees whose large, brown fruit clung to the trunk like little koala bears, their highly perfumed interior made up of sweet, sticky segments. As a mango tree yields five hundred or more fruit, there were far too many for the family to consume.

In keeping with the custom of the time, Purna auctioned the mango and jackfruit trees – for the season only – to a local 'khatik' in the bazaar. Khatiks were merchants who traded mainly in foodstuffs but also dabbled in businesses such as construction and money-lending. Before the trees became his property, the khatik promised a few hundred mangoes and a couple of jackfruit to the family.

It was now his responsibility to guard the crop. He organized relay teams of young sons and workers to mind the trees. The minder spent all day in the garden, chasing away urchins who aimed their slings at the fruit overhanging the boundary wall. He alleviated his boredom by playing with the children of the house. Or he chattered away to the gardener as he followed him around. Occasionally, he brought along a companion to play marbles, cards or a game of pebbles. At night, he slept under a tree on a rush mat.

Great rivalry existed between the khatiks. Minders in neighbouring gardens, working for different khatiks, relieved the monotony by trading insults. And of course, people often let their neighbours know, through their servants, that *their* khatik was the highest bidder in the area.

Sometimes, a storm at night stripped the trees of their weaker fruit. Green mangoes bounced off mosquito nets and the next morning found the lawn littered with unripe fruit. These, being no good to the khatik, ended up as pickles and chutneys. After de-stoning the fruit, Kanchan mixed them with mustard oil, salt and spices. She packed them into large, earthenware jars and left them out in the sun to 'cook' for a week or two. Or she produced sweet 'Kashmiri' chutney by boiling the sliced mangoes in a spicy sugar and raisin syrup.

The overwhelming smell of ripe fruit in the summer air heralded harvest time. The khatik arrived with helpers, baskets and a large handcart. His helpers climbed the trees and, using long bamboos topped with hooks, coaxed the mangoes off the tree. A sharp knife separated the jackfruit from their tree trunks. They loaded the fruit-filled baskets onto the hand-cart and wheeled it away to the bazaar. Bare fruit trees usually signified the end of summer and the breaking of the monsoon rains. Next year the khatiks would bid for the trees again.

Kanchan, under the mango trees

49

10
PLAYING FIELDS

The houses in Lukergunj were built around a field which was really just a large square of waste ground. Kanchan Villa, being on a corner site, had a little side wicket in the boundary wall that led to the field. This scraggy and dusty plot of land served a multitude of uses. In the far right corner a little two-roomed club-house offered basic gymnastic and table-tennis facilities. Early in the morning young men often worked out on the parallel bars outside the clubhouse, their lithe, well-oiled bodies glistening in the sun.

Sometimes, in the winter sunshine, the local free school held an outdoor class in the field, the eager young pupils sitting cross-legged in rows, reciting the alphabet and tables in a sing-song manner.

In the tranquil dawn of summer, Purna and Kanchan joined other residents on their morning constitution around the field. Some strolled while chewing on neem twigs to cleanse mouth and teeth, spitting out the bitter juice. Still in their dressing gowns, they greeted each other and exchanged pleasantries before returning home to breakfast.

Occasionally, the sound of tinkling bells and Hindu hymns, from an early-morning prayer meeting, drifted on the gentle morning breeze.

Early evenings saw the arrival of ayahs with their little charges. While the children played, the ayahs squatted in groups, gossiping about their employers. At dusk, snack hawkers descended on the field. They sold peanuts and horse gram which they roasted, spiced and packed into little newspaper cones; chaat – a menu of spicy snacks and drinks; kulfi – ice-lolly made from milk, rose-water and pistachio nuts; peanut brittle and seasonal fruit. Families often called a vendor into their garden and after 'feeding' them he returned to the field. The smoke from the peanut-seller's barbecue kept midges at bay – one of the advantages of hanging around him. Otherwise, the midges formed a buzzing column over one's head and the superstition was that they followed those who did not say their prayers. The truth, of course, was that midges found the scent of some hair oils more attractive than others.

Once or twice a week the field hosted a football match between local teams. Clouds of dust billowed up as a grubby ball was furiously kicked around by bare feet, amid much excited shouting. As a teenager, Sunny played football with a local team, often returning home with minor injuries. But his football days came to an end the day his team challenged the soldiers of the 25th Field Battery. In the hurly-burly of the game, Sunny was kicked in the mouth by a heavy army boot. His team-mates carried him home, with a bloody mouth and wobbly teeth. The dentist managed to save his teeth but they remained badly discoloured for the rest of his life.

Anu learned to cycle on the field, Prashad running alongside her to help her up every time she fell off. In later years, while Purna had his morning shave, Molly seized the barber's cycle to ride it round and round the field.

When Anu was twelve she 'grew up', as it was politely put, ahead of her peers. The sanitary protection she used was bulky and uncomfortable. For the first few months the child wept at this 'affliction' and could not understand why her sisters and friends were free of it. She cursed being born a girl as her mother told her boys didn't 'suffer' from it. The worst part was when Purna banned her from going to the field any more. As soon as girls reached puberty they were 'withdrawn' from the field. They were now considered ladies to be protected from the appreciative glances of the young men out there. The fact that some of these lads were their playmates was not up for discussion. As their entire social life until now, had revolved round the field, this sudden turn-about was hard to accept.

Anu watched longingly as her friends played in the field while she sat on the verandah reading 'War and Peace'. It nurtured her love of reading but, being little more than a child herself, she found the rule confusing. It helped when, in the next year or two, her peers caught up with her. They were no longer allowed to frequent the field either. Instead, they formally called on each other at home, as young ladies did.

Kanchan Villa, with the field beyond it.

When the Sarkars moved from West Khusru Bagh to Lukergunj, it was a long way to the route of the Moharrum procession. But Kanchan Villa was closer to another festival – Durga Puja. The ten-day extravaganza, venerating the Hindu goddess, Durga, was held in the field beside the house.

Sunny acted with local young men in the religious drama every night. The stage was within a shamianah – a marquee constructed from thick cotton fabric with bold geometric appliqués in blinding reds, blues and yellows – whose length was divided in two, by a big fishing net. It separated the men from the women – purdah, 1930s style. Kanchan took the girls to see the concert from 9 pm to midnight. They removed their sandals at the entrance and settled down on the red and blue striped cotton durries to watch the evening's performance of music, song and drama.

On the last day, at the first sound of clashing cymbals, Anu and her sisters ran out to the gate to watch goddess Durga's procession. The demonic goddess, dressed in black with red tongue hanging out of her mouth, demanded an offering from every house. Refusal meant a curse on the family. By sunset, the procession had reached the river and a large throng had gathered to watch Durga meet her watery end.

Close to Lukergunj was Lascombe's Field. British and Anglo-Indian families occupied the houses along one side of Lascombe's Field – among them, the Gores, Wasdells and MacPhails, an Anglo-Indian family, affectionately known as 'The Macs'. Their outhouses were occupied by domestic workers employed in homes within walking distance of the area.

Lascombe's Field was dominated by the offices of the local newspaper, 'The Leader' – an English-language paper that wielded a great deal of influence in the ongoing struggle for Independence. The press compound also held a small post office. A grubby jar of glue sat on the sill of its little window, for use with stamps.

A concrete slippery slide outside the press offices was a favourite with local children. The Sarkars' ayah sometimes took them to the Leader Press to play. It was a nice change from the Lukergunj field.

11
HELPING HANDS

Purna and Kanchan brought along their little team of helpers when they moved to Lukergunj. There was Raghu, the mali, who patiently watered the garden with a battered old watering can. His wife, the cook, was simply referred to as Raghu Bibi – wife of Raghu. Long after her husband died, Raghu Bibi, a bent and toothless old harridan, remained firmly ensconced in the bosom of the family.

The mehri, Kanti, cleaned the house and was often accompanied to work by her toddler daughter, Tara. Kanti was particularly attractive with almond eyes and thick, glossy hair, carelessly knotted at the nape of her neck. Although married, it was no secret that she was also the 'woman' of an Englishman called Mr Whitby. Many Indian maidservants ended up in this situation, often bearing Anglo-Indian children. After Independence, when Mr Whitby returned to England, he sent Kanti the princely sum of £1 every Christmas. Until the 1960s Kanti would proudly present her English cheque for Kanchan to cash.

Devi, the ayah, helped Kanchan with the children. Her husband was the grass-cutter. In the absence of a lawn-mower, the grass was cut by hand with a scythe. Devi's husband came whenever the mali decided the grass was too long. He took the grass-cuttings to the bazaar to be sold as fodder. The couple lived in the same colony as Kanti – a long row of outhouses at Lascombe's Field, occupied by those in menial jobs. Their little son, Prashad, also came to work with his mother and played with Tara under the trees while their mothers swept, swabbed, dusted and tended the children. Many years later, the two caused a scandal by eloping when Tara's marriage to someone else was arranged.

Gaazi, the sweeper, came from the lowest caste and cleaned all the toilets in the area. Twice a day, he entered from the back door of the toilet, emptied and cleaned the commodes and washed the floor with Phenyl. He used a big broom – like a witch's broom, but without the long staff – to sweep around the house and under the trees. The action of sweeping large areas for long periods of time gave him a bent back and bow legs. Gaazi only ever wore a loin cloth and turban and in winter, a moth-eaten woollen shawl around his scrawny shoulders.

The punkha wali was employed to activate the punkha – a deep fabric frill suspended from a pole running along the middle of the ceiling. A heavy rope attached to the pole pulled the frill to and fro, creating a light breeze. The punkha-wali squatted on the floor, resting her back against a wall, and pulled the punkha back and forth in a trance-like state. If she dropped off, she was rudely awakened by Prashad flapping a live chicken in her face.

Holly's little friend Beryl, daughter of 'The Macs', told her that she and her siblings took turns pulling the punkha all day to keep their mother cool. If they faltered they got the lash of Mrs Mac's tongue – anyone who lived in Lascombe's Field could confirm this.

Apart from these full-time helpers, there were others who worked on a regular basis. Once a week, the dhobi came with his donkey to collect the dirty laundry, bringing last week's washed clothes and linen. Kanchan recorded the list of clothes to be laundered in her dhobi book, ticking off the ones that had been returned. The dhobi spread a bed sheet on the floor, placed the soiled clothes along its length, folded the two sides over and knotted both ends. The sausage-shaped bundle was draped over the back of the donkey and it trotted off, led by its master to the dhobis' colony. The dhobi joined others at the river and washed the clothes, beating the heavily-soiled ones against smooth rocks. Lines of colourful clothes and saris festooned the river banks like festive bunting. Rice starch stiffened cotton garments and household linen. If the job of starching fell to one of the dhobi's children, everything was stiffened – towels felt like sandpaper. 'Blue' was used to enhance whites, which were often returned with streaks of blue. A heavy iron, filled with charcoal, pressed the clothes before they were neatly folded and returned on the appointed day of the week. The dhobi had a little code for each family – a pattern of small dots in indelible ink on an unseen part of the garment.

The residents of Lukergunj employed a night watchman to patrol the area at night. He walked around the field, loudly clearing his throat and calling, 'Sleepers beware!' In keeping with his status as security man, he designed himself a policeman-like uniform of khaki shirt and trousers and Gandhi cap. Naturally, he always carried a baton. His presence was particularly reassuring on summer nights, when most people slept outdoors.

When Prashad was five years old, his mother became gravely ill. Realising her life was nearing its end she asked Kanchan to care for her son after she was gone. When Devi died, Prashad continued to live with his father in Lascombe Field's outhouses but came to Kanchan Villa each day with Kanti to 'work', ever responsive to Purna's call of 'Boy!'

He started out by tending the poultry. Next to the bathing house was a row of chicken coops for Purna's poultry. On arrival at Kanchan Villa each morning, Prashad could not wait to enter the coops to look for eggs, particularly the tiny one laid by the oldest bird, 'Gargosh' (Past It). He presented the eggs to Raghu Bibi who gave him a bucket of shredded vegetable peel, mixed with corn and grain. He scattered the feed before the birds and watched over them while they clucked and pecked, scaring off predatory crows with a stick. When feeding time was over, he shepherded the birds to the field for exercise. After lunch, he swept up the feathers to make soft bedding for the birds. Before he left for home, he ensured the birds were safely locked in for the night.

One evening, Prashad forgot to close the coop door. As the family slept peacefully under the mango trees, Gargosh flew out to Purna's bed, fluttering, squawking and pecking at his mosquito net. He followed the bird back to the coop to discover a snake slithering its way towards the eggs. Picking up a stick, Purna killed it with a sharp whack. He settled Gargosh and the other birds back into the coop before returning to bed. The next day Prashad was not only sorry for endangering the birds but also afraid of coming upon a snake in the coop.

Over the years, Prashad progressed from poultry-tender to Man Friday to self-appointed Head of the Household Cavalry. He was such an intrinsic part of the family that it was his hand Kanchan was holding when she died, at the age of ninety.

Prashad with Dinky, the first grandchild

12

TRADE ROUTES

Before he left for work each morning, Purna went to the market to buy meat. He did not trust anyone else to choose meat that was fresh and from the right animal. Some Muslim butchers had licenses to slaughter cows – they mostly sold to British and Anglo-Indians. Being early, Purna had the pick of fresh lamb. The butcher was one of the few tradesmen who did not come to the door every day.

The doodh wallah came at first light and went straight to the kitchen where he filled a couple of pots from his milk churn, under Ragu Bibi's watchful eye. If the milk was not frothy enough, she accused him of watering it. If he poured it from a height, she complained he was trying to whip up a froth. Kanchan was confident the milk came straight from the cow. After it was boiled twice, a thick layer of cream formed over it. Pointing this out to Raghi Bibi would have been in vain – the cook loved her daily altercation with the milkman.

Like all Bengalis, the Sarkars were keen fish-eaters – all except Anu. She hated the smell and did not have the patience to pick out the fine bones. Often Kanchan hailed a fish-seller as he or she walked round Lukergunj with a basket on the head, calling 'Fresh fish! Hilsa today! (or whatever fish had been caught in the river that morning). Kanchan checked the fish's gills for freshness and looked for a bellyful of roe, before buying it. Raghu Bibi descaled it on a hasli – a curved, upright blade on a wooden base – before cutting it into steaks to cook.

The family grew its own fruit and vegetables but looked out for the onion and potato vendors. They usually brought their wares on a handcart, laden with shiny-skinned onions or mounds of muddy potatoes. Kanchan bought foods they did not grow themselves, from hawkers. A particular favourite was an old woman called Jugni. Kanchan always tried to buy something from her because her basket of wares was so small, she did not earn much in a day. When Jugni abruptly stopped calling, Kanchan was worried. Eventually she asked another seller.

'Jugni died three days ago,' he said.

'But she wasn't ill,' said Kanchan, 'I bought fruit from her four days ago and she seemed fine.'

'I know. We were all very shocked. She died so suddenly.'

A few days later Kanchan could not believe her eyes when Jugni turned up with her basket of vegetables on her head.

'I thought you were dead!' cried Kanchan.

'I did die, but God said to me, "Jugni, it was not you I asked for, I wanted Jugnu." So he sent me back.'

'You saw God? And spoke to him?'

'Yes, he was as close as you are to me.'

'What did he look like?'

'O very clean. His turban was so white it glowed!'

'What was heaven like?'

'Beautiful! Rows and rows of shiny purple aubergines, huge pumpkins and bright red tomatoes. God has a lovely garden. I've never seen anything like it on this earth.'

Whoever poor Jugnu was, Kanchan was glad he had swapped places with Jugni and given her a few more years on earth.

Some door-to-door sellers and tradesman only appeared in the winter months. The jam-'jaley' wallah sold ... jam and jelly. He rode a bicycle with bags hanging from every part, the sound of clinking bottles heralding his arrival. Apart from a fine selection of fruit preserves, he also sold guava cheese – a sweet, wine-coloured block with a distinctive guava flavour. The jam-jaley wallah refused to divulge his 'secret British recipes' despite Raghu Bibi's wily attempts to learn how to produce the jams herself. For elevenses, Kanchan spread jam or jelly on chapattis and rolled them up for the children. The guava cheese, being more expensive, was a special treat.

Winter also brought the dhunai wallah out on the streets. His service was essential to most families, either before or after the cold season. When engaged by Kanchan, the dhunai wallah found a sunny spot in the garden and settled down for the day. All the family's razais – satin quilts – were ripped open and their lumpy cotton contents emptied onto a clean sheet. The dhunai wallah passed handfuls of cotton through the strings of a harp-like instrument, dispersing the lumps and looking for rogue cotton-seeds in the silky fleece. He twanged away while Kanchan had the quilt covers washed and hung out to dry. When he was finished, a mountain of fluffy cotton lay on the sheet. His job was done. A servant hastened to the bazaar to return with a silai walli. She took the place vacated by the dhunai wallah and stuffed the cotton back into the freshly laundered covers. Producing a bodkin from her bag, she hand-quilted all the razais until they looked new again.

The mochi called regularly to mend the family's shoes. From his worn and dirty canvas bag he produced an anvil, hammer and chisel. With his chisel he cut new soles or heels from rolls of leather. He nailed these onto the old shoes or sewed them on with strong waxed twine, finishing off with a brisk rub of Cherry Blossom shoe polish.

When Raghu Bibi complained that the silver interiors of her copper and brass cooking vessels were fading, it was time to call the kalai wallah. He found a suitable spot near the kitchen, dug a shallow hole and lit a charcoal fire in it. A pot was heated over the fire. When it was sufficiently hot, the kalai wallah swiftly rubbed a length of silver wire inside it. With a handful of cotton filaments he quickly swirled around inside the pot and it was good as new again. Ragh Bibi was pleased – she could see her reflection in the shiny re-silvered interiors, however distorted the image. She was equally pleased when the choori-dhar wallah sharpened her kitchen knives, leaving her with a fine set of cutting tools.

Sometimes Kanchan exchanged her old saris for cooking pots. The borders of her silk saris were woven from gold or silver thread. When the silk perished, she set aside the sari for the bartan wallah. With an experienced eye, he gauged the precious metal content of the borders and offered Kanchan steel or copper pots of equivalent value.

Every year the family watched out for the kursi-binai wallah. He arrived with a roll of cane over his shoulder and a small bag of tools. For hours he beavered away, re-weaving the wicker seats of all the chairs. Similarly, the charpai-binai wallah re-wove the string cots, or 'charpoys', on a regular basis. With a sharp knife, he carefully cut around inside the frame to remove the old matting intact, so he could sell it to the homeless to sleep on.

Once a year the varnish-paint wallah smartened up the wrought-iron gate and varnished tired furniture. As he grew older, his paints became thinner. Eventually he used such a diluted paint that, at the first rain, the maroon paint ran down the bars of the gate and settled in red puddles under it. Purna bided his time. The next time he heard 'Varneeesh! Paint!' at the gate, he let the pet dog loose on the man. The little terrier was harmless but the furious yapping frightened him away and 'Varneeesh!' was never heard at the gate again.

At the end of each month the ruddi-kagaz wallah presented himself at the kitchen door. He bought all the empty bottles and tins from Kanchan, as well as bundles of old newspapers, by weight.

After the school term, he bought the children's old copy books which were made into paper bags and sold to shops.

The children's favourite hawkers were the two box wallahs. The first carried a zinc trunk on his head which he unpacked on the verandah, to the delight of Anu and her sisters. He unrolled a little mat on which he systematically laid out the contents of his trunk. There were buttons, laces and ribbons; hairpins, clips and safety-pins; Brylcreem and hair oils; pomades and Vaseline; Vicks, Aspro and balms; shoe-laces and boot polish; small plastic toys and locks; glass bangles and cheap, jangly earrings and necklaces; kohl for the eyes, bindis for the forehead and red powder for the parting in the hair; jars of Himalayan Snow vanishing cream and tins of Himalayan Bouquet talcum powder; and red nail varnish – *always* red nail varnish.

The second boxwallah was more up-market. Chinaman Chow-Chow brought beautiful silks all the way from China to the door. He also imported delicate necklaces made from jade, opal, jet and other semi-precious stones. As he rode his bicycle through the streets, with a cigar between his teeth, children ran alongside chanting:

'Chin, Chin, Chinaman,

Chow, chow, chow,

Riding on a bicycle

Bow, wow, wow!

Chin, Chin, Chinaman,

Smoking a cigar

Riding on an elephant

Ha! Ha! Ha!'

At Kanchan Villa, Anu and her sisters excitedly gathered round him as he shook out his crepe de Chines and brocades with a flourish. His visit to the Sarkars' house was well worth his time – Kanchan always bought a lot of his stock for her four daughters. One Christmas she bought up his entire roll of white silk organza, printed with delicate orange flowers, in the fond hope that no one else would have the same dresses as her daughters. At the Christmas service in the cathedral, they were surprised to see their neighbour, Doris Finch, in an identical fabric. The Chinaman had called to her house before Kanchan Villa.

13
INDIAN CHRISTIANS

Religion was an important part of family life in India and the Sarkars were no exception. While Purna's family were earlier converts, Kanchan's father converted to Christianity as a young man in the Calcutta Secretariat. Her brother Dhiren's moving Bengali hymns were sung in the city's Christ Church.

In Allahabad the family attended All Saints Cathedral, close to the railway station. Sir William Emerson – famous for Calcutta's Victoria Memorial – designed the Gothic style building in 1870. The locals referred to it as 'patthar girja', stone church, to distinguish it from other churches in the city as it was built of white granite with red stone dressings. On Sunday mornings the family rode to the cathedral in Jagannath's tonga.

Anu first became aware of the difference between Protestants and Roman Catholics when she was in the nursery section of St Anne's Convent. While all the children followed the Corpus Christi procession to St Joseph's Church, only the Catholic children were seated in the main body. The remaining children were crowded into a small room, off the vestry, from where they could neither see nor hear anything. A stern nun kept the fidgeting children quiet through the forty-five minute mass.

Things were not much different in Anu's own church. Although converted by the British, Indians were required to sit in the rear pews of the church as the main body was occupied by British families, many of whom had reserved pews. A large number of pews were taken up by the army based at Allahabad Fort. After them, came the Anglo-Indians and last of all, the Indians. Anu was quick to note the advantage of this seating system. On ceremonial days her family got a good view of the standard bearers and regimental bands as they assembled at the west door, for the procession down the aisle. It was also easy for the family to leave after the service, before the aisles clogged up with worshippers trying to get out.

On Sunday afternoons Anu and her siblings walked to Lascombe's Field, and joined local Christian children in the McGoverns' home, where a deaconess from the cathedral conducted Sunday school.

At bedtime, the family assembled in Purna's study for prayers. Kanchan recited a long prayer in Bengali, careful not to omit the name of any relative, before they united in the Lord's Prayer. Her faith gave her a calm that astonished her husband and children. Never was it more evident than the night of the earthquake. The family had hardly moved into Kanchan Villa when an earthquake rattled the bones of the city. As the terrified children ran out of the house, Purna rushed around, filling his pockets with Kanchan's jewellery and any money he could find. When he joined the others in the garden he noticed Kanchan had brought her harmonium out with her. As they watched their new house sway from side to side, Kanchan began to play the harmonium and sing a hymn. Eventually the others joined in. They sang hymns all night long until police vans gave them the all clear. The next day, when they heard that Allahabad Railway station had collapsed, Purna marvelled at his wife's fortitude in the face of impending disaster – she had sung praises to God all the way through an earthquake.

For a while Kanchan, like many Indian Christians, was enthralled by an evangelist called Jeevarathanam. The preacher travelled from city to city, calling on the faithful to follow Jesus. During his eagerly awaited annual visit to Allahabad, he filled a massive shamianah with his devoted followers. The bearded preacher appeared on stage and shouted, 'Are you ready?'

'We are ready!' the crowd roared back.

He then led them in a rousing hymn about being ready to follow Jesus. After a long and rambling sermon, several collection plates were passed around. Kanchan took her daughters to the meetings but Purna refused to accompany them. He suspected the preacher was a fraud. He may have been right. One year Jeevarathanam did not turn up in Allahabad. The rumour was that he had decamped with the money – no one knew where.

However, this did not put Kanchan off all preachers. When she heard 'God is Love!' at the gate, she rushed out and welcomed the catechist into her home. The saffron-robed Guru Prashad walked from house to house, teaching the Gospel. He was respected, loved and treated as a truly holy man. Even Purna agreed that Guru Prashad was a man of God.

On the 20th of February 1937, Anu was confirmed in the cathedral. In the Anglican tradition, her First Communion followed four days later, on St Mathias' Day. To mark the occasion the bishop gave her a little red book – 'My Prayer Book for Women and Girls.' It had an introduction by two Archbishops of Canterbury and took the reader through the communion service with additional prayers for 'Camp' and 'Tent'. In later pages it advised the following:

'Remember that most men still look up to women and will for their sakes try to live clean and honourable lives. Friendship with a girl is often the greatest power for good in a man's life.

'On the other hand, never make yourself cheap; know no man without a proper introduction. As to dress, a girl is right to wear nice clothes and to make the best of her appearance; but to choose "flashy" things and to "make up" conspicuously is simply to ask for trouble, and to attract the wrong sort of man.'

Anu hand-wrote additions into the prayer book, including Anima Christi and St. Patrick's Breastplate. (Little did she know, at the time, that she would end her days in the land of St. Patrick.)

The Sarkars' friends were mostly Indian Christians – like the Shaws, who lived by Gudiya Talao or Doll's Lake. Anu and her sisters particularly enjoyed visiting during the Hindu Festival of Dolls when little girls and young women, bathed dolls in Gudiya Talao in a ritual of fertility. Jacob Shaw was a clerk in the Christian Tract & Book Society while his wife was a midwife in Dufferin Hospital. Despite a tag of skin inside her right elbow, which

71

prevented her from straightening her arm, she was one of the most respected midwives in the hospital. When the Maharani of Rewa was expecting her first baby, Dufferin Hospital recommended Nurse Shaw to the royal family. Leading up to the birth, she moved into the palace at Rewa. In time she delivered a healthy heir to the throne and went on to deliver all the royal babies. Each time, she returned to Allahabad laden with gems and jewels given to her by the grateful royals.

Many Indian Christians lived in an estate belonging to a nawab, simply called 'Nawab Sahib's compound'. Within high boundary walls were extensive gardens, surrounded by buildings in which suites of rooms were rented out. The Rufus family lived in one such suite – the four daughters were friendly with the Sarkar girls, being close in age. The gardens in Nawab Sahib's Compound were used for social events organised by his Christian tenants. It was a favoured venue for wedding receptions, which were well-attended as they provided the perfect opportunity for Indian Christian parents to find suitable matches for their children.

On ceremonial occasions, Indian Christians joined British families in Alfred Park – the largest park in the city. Dominated by statues of King George V and Queen Victoria, it was originally called Company Bagh by the East India Company. The Police Band provided rousing music as uniforms and medals, voile dresses and hats mingled with dhotis and kurtas, saris and parasols. Kanchan took pride in dressing her little daughters in smart frocks and hats from the exclusive British firm, Whiteway Laidlaw. Their shoes, of course, came from Mr Fookson.

The Allahabad Purdah Club was set up to encourage social interaction between sophisticated Indian women and their British counterparts. Kanchan was invited to join but declined, as her Christian religion and Purna's career gave her sufficient opportunity to mix with British women. Besides, the family had many friends and Kanchan rarely socialised without her husband.

14
FESTIVAL FEVER

Christmas in the Sarkar household was preceded by weeks of hectic activity. The annual white-washing of the house meant days of upheaval and disruption. White-washers painted the walls with clumsy brushes and lime solution, while their supervisor smoked his bidi and ordered them around. Things were moved from their original places. Things went missing. When Purna's pocket watch went missing, he was perplexed – he had placed it on his desk a minute ago. While hunting for it, he noticed the supervisor's fidgety behaviour. Purna stared at the man for a minute then, acting on impulse, he reached up and swiped the turban off his head. As the flying turban unfurled, the pocket watch flew out of its folds.

The British firm, Whiteway Laidlaw, supplied the children's Christmas Day outfits. As Kanchan enjoyed sewing she spent hours at her little Singer machine, producing dresses and bonnets for the girls to wear over the festive season. Mr Fookson measured their little feet and promised them shoes for the day. Purna trailed the whole family round the bazaar as they excitedly chose socks, ribbons, hair clips and other accessories. When Anu started wearing saris, she once chose a sari that was dearer than the one chosen by Kanchan. To the bewilderment of the shop-keeper, Purna made Anu return it for one less expensive than her mother's, despite Kanchan's protests. His wife had to have the best – always.

The season brought a surreptitious tradesman to the door – the Hunter-Meat wallah. Careful not to be overheard by the Hindu helpers in the house, Kanchan took the vendor aside to order a side of salted beef. The butcher spent the next two weeks marinating the meat in lemon and black rock salt, before slow-roasting it. The beef was delivered to Kanchan Villa, heavily disguised as an innocent parcel. Despite the cloak-and-dagger, it was an open secret that most Christian families served Hunter Meat over the Christmas period.

A week before Christmas, Purna went to the market and returned with a coolie carrying a basket of fruit on his head. Kanchan spread the apples, oranges, bananas, guavas and pineapples on open shelves in the dining-room, from where their sweet smell pervaded the house.

With Christmas nearly upon them, Purna and Kanchan went secret-shopping for the children's presents and clothes for the servants. Three days before Christmas, the cook, helped by the girls (Sunny was barred for eating the almonds and raisins), sieved flour, washed raisins, blanched almonds, chopped candied peel and halved glacé cherries in preparation for cake-making. The next day the baker arrived with helpers and settled on the long side verandah. In huge bowls they whipped the eggs, blended butter, flour and sugar, combining all the ingredients with the fruit and nuts. A generous splash of vanilla essence completed the cake mixture. They loaded the bowls on a tonga and rode to the bakery. A servant followed in a rickshaw with two sterilised tin trunks. The bakery was booked for the day by Purna – Indian Christian families each reserved a day for their Christmas baking. The servant spent the next couple of hours at the bakery until the cakes were done. In the evening he returned with the cakes in the two tin trunks. Amongst the thirty cakes were small ones in Polson's butter tins, baked especially for the children. The cakes were stored until Christmas Day, when ten or more cakes were cut for friends and neighbours calling to wish the family Happy Christmas. The rest were eaten everyday until Epiphany.

Christmas was not complete without the typically Indian Christian snacks of gauja and gujia. The former was made from thick, sweetened dough, rolled out, cut into diamond shapes and deep-fried. Gujias were
little puff pastries with a sweet filling. Kanchan set aside a day for the production of gaujas and gujias which she packed into tall tin canisters. They were served at tea-time, over the festive season.

The family attended Christmas service at the cathedral and on their return, the servants lined up for baksheesh. In addition to money they got clothes, groceries, fruit and a Christmas cake each. When the family lived in West Khusru Bagh, they enjoyed the festivities organised by their British and Anglo-Indian neighbours. The children eagerly awaited the tin pot band – a ragged group of musicians, dressed in colourful costumes. They sang, danced and played on battered instruments outside every house. These retired barrack workers and domestics composed verses from phrases picked up from the B.O.Rs (British Other Ranks).

'Chumping Charlie, there's my boy

Good for nothing, you're my joy!'

Taking 'You're good for nothing, Charlie my boy,' as a compliment, the ditty earned them good baksheesh at Christmas.

A white-haired woman, in brightly patterned skirt twirled her garish scarf as she sang 'Degi, Degi' – her version of the popular 'Daisy, Daisy'. When stuck for words, she made up her own – 'Irish myrish' for stylish marriage and so on.

Mary, the sweepress, had a song too.

'Mary, Mary, jharoo le kar aao

'Paat saaf karo, chota geet gao.'

(Mary, Mary bring along your broom

Clean the chamber pot, sing a small tune.)

On Boxing Day the churches held individual sports events, with races, prizes and goodies for the children. The Railway Club held its sports on the expansive lawns of Khusru Bagh. Purna took the family to the event every year. Only railway families (mostly British and Anglo-Indian) were allowed to participate in the sports but other children enjoyed the food, elephant rides and merry-go-rounds.

The highlight of the season for Indian Christians was the united churches' picnic at Sangam – the confluence of the Ganges and Jamuna. Tottering onto several rocking boats, the church group, accompanied by helpers carrying large dekchis of food, rowed down one of the rivers.

They pointed excitedly to the Maharani of Rewa's luxurious boat, permanently moored at Sangam, should the royal lady wish to take a dip in the holy river. Upon arrival at their chosen site, the helpers lit wood fires and cooked, while picnickers frolicked on the sandy bank of the river. They sat on durries and ate their lunch, before organising competitive games between the churches. Then they sang together, starting off with hymns and ending up with more popular music, clapping to the rhythm. At sunset they loaded up the boats again and rowed back up the river. Such occasions inculcated a sense of unity between the churches and camaraderie between Indian Christian families.

The euphoria of Christmas was in complete contrast to the next season in the Christian calendar. During Lent, Kanchan only served vegetarian meals. Being dedicated fish and meat-eaters, this was a big sacrifice for the family. Apart from the act of denying themselves, any saving made on their food bill was given to the church. On Good Friday, the older members fasted until sunset. The whole family attended the three-hour devotion at the cathedral from noon until 3 p.m. While Kanchan, with covered and bowed head, was entirely absorbed by the Stations of the Cross, Purna, feeling for the children, sneaked them out once or twice during the afternoon. He treated them to cold drinks and sherbet from the food vendors who besieged gates of churches during Christian festivals. Refreshed, the children tiptoed into the church again for the next station of the cross. Back home, they were required to be quiet and contemplate the events of the first Good Friday. 'Barabas' by Kanchan's favourite author, Marie Corelli, was passed around for the older children to read, particularly the chapter on the crucifixion of Christ.

This sombre mood was soon broken by the arrival of Easter. After morning service at the cathedral, the family rode in Jagannath's tonga to Civil Lines, where Purna bought Easter eggs for the children from the confectionery shop in the fashionable Barnett's Hotel. The shells were made from marzipan and the insides filled with caramels and toffees. They went home to a lunch of goose curry – the unfortunate bird having been picked from Purna's flock.

On Easter Monday all the churches in the city united to hold a mela (fair), mainly for Indian Christians. Muirabad Church, having the largest grounds, hosted the Easter mela, with participating churches each manning a stall. Apart from food, drink and games, there were swings for the children – among them the 'hurdy-gurdy', an indigenous version of the ferris wheel with four wooden chairs. Two burly men manually spun the large cart-wheel and the swinging chairs creaked and groaned to accompanying squeals of delight.

After the mela, rows of long cotton durries covered the dusty ground on which fair-goers sat cross-legged and ate from throw-away bowls made from leaves. Professional cooks prepared the meal on the grounds, in large pots on log fires. The menu usually consisted of pulao rice, chicken curry, a vegetable dish, raita, puri and a salad of diced onion, tomato and chilli. For dessert they had carrot halwa or syrupy Indian sweetmeats.

The quiet gap between Easter and Christmas was more than filled by the Hindu and Muslim festivals in which the family participated with their non-Christian friends. There were many noisy and colourful celebrations to enjoy and the year passed quickly.

15
RELATIVE FREQUENCY

Kanchan Villa always had a steady stream of visiting relatives, the favourite being Kanchan's mother. Anu's first recollection of 'Didima' (grandmother) was when, at the age of four, she went to Calcutta. She was puzzled to find her widowed grandmother only ever dressed in a white sari, stripped of jewellery. Standing on the verandah of the Pandey family home, Anu saw a bus for the first time in her life. The persistent blowing of a bus's horn brought Purna out to investigate. He found his daughter with arms outstretched, standing in the path of the bus, preventing it from pulling away from the stop. The amused passengers applauded when Purna swept the child up in his arms. Even the scowling bus driver managed a smile.

Anu was fascinated by trams, with their horizontal steering wheels.

'Look, Daddy,' she cried excitedly, 'the man's making ice-cream!'

When Didima visited the family in Allahabad, she came laden with the goodies that Kanchan missed. In matkas – earthen pots – the size of water-melons, she brought Bengali sweets, coconut jaggery made from palm sugar, salted fish and spiced king prawns. She also brought little 3" chinnia bananas from her own garden.

While the other children pounced on the matkas with delight, Holly was put off by the smell of fish. She marched up to her grandmother, grabbed her by her white sari and dragged her out of the house.

'Shada' (white)!' she yelled, 'take your smelly food and go away!'

'Fine,' replied Didima, 'I'll take away my smelly fish but what about my sweets and fruit and toys? I'll have to take them, too.'

For her owns needs Didima brought along her tin of gul. She rubbed this mixture of charcoal and tobacco on her mostly toothless gums each morning, both to cleanse her mouth as well as deaden any pain in surviving teeth.

Didima draped her sari in the Bengali style. She tried to keep the hem clean by hitching it up and tucking into the waistband, leaving her with a calf-length sari. The sight of her pale bow-legs was an irritation to Anu who described them as 'crooked, white nails'. After that, Didima was affectionately referred to as 'Crooked White Nails'. Purna, regretful that his children never knew his mother, was devoted to his mother-in-law. He remembered with sadness how he hastened home to Calcutta as his mother lay dying. 'Purna... Purna', she whispered repeatedly, aware that only one child was missing from her bedside. She slipped away minutes before he reached her – a sadness he always carried in his heart.

Relatives from Bengal

There was anguish in Kanchan's family when her sister, Arulata, died at childbirth. Her baby, christened Lily, was largely brought up by Didima. Often when Anu's grandmother visited she was accompanied by Lily. Sometimes the little girl's jealousy at her grandmother's love for her cousins got the better of her. When Anu and her sisters found their toys and hair clips mysteriously broken, there was no doubt as to who the culprit was, but Didima would not hear a word against Lily.

Kanchan's brother, the cigar-chomping Dhiren, frequently stopped by in Allahabad on his way from Calcutta to Delhi, on business. A talented poet and musician, he composed hymns in Bengali that were sung in Christ Church, Calcutta. At family prayers before bedtime, he played Kanchan's harmonium as they all sang his hymns.

Her other siblings visited too – all except her second brother. He married a Hindu girl and moved to Benares, severing contact with his family. Some years later, they heard he had died and was hastily cremated. As his family was not informed, it raised suspicions of foul play, the finger pointing at his wife.

Kanchan's favourite sister, Bijulata, had thick hair down to her knees. She lay on a string cot with her hair over the edge for Kanchan to wash. She stayed in that position until her hair was dry, otherwise wet hair down her back gave her a cold. Purna loved spoiling her with fancy toiletries from the bazaar. To the consternation of her brothers, Bijulata fell in love with a Hindu neighbour. When Purna heard they had barred her from meeting the young man, he offered to arrange their marriage in Allahabad. But Bijuli lost her nerve as well as the will to live. One winter's day, she washed her hair and stood out in the cold air, until she caught a chill. The cold turned to pneumonia and she took to her bed, telling her family that she would rise from it no more. Kanchan and Purna were devastated at what they considered her 'suicide'. Kanchan blamed her brothers and never forgave them.

Purna's sisters' visits were greeted with trepidation. His family, less traditional than Kanchan's, allowed the girls to make their own choices. They grew up to be strong and domineering. His sisters, all older than Kanchan, bossed her about when they visited. Shiu, after her divorce from Mr Staines, lost no time in finding her next husband. She targeted a doctor in the Calcutta hospital and after a respectable period, married Dr Sengupta.

On one of her many visits to Allahabad, Shui sat 'sewing a fine seam', occasionally dipping into a platter of Indian sweetmeats beside her. When the five-year-old Anu reached for a sweet, Shui picked up her heavy tailoring scissors and brought them down on the child's knuckles. At lunch Purna noticed that his little daughter was unable to lift a tumbler of water. On discovering the reason for her bruised and swollen knuckles, he put an end, once and for all, to his sister's bullying – she was no longer welcome at Kanchan Villa. Shui left in disgrace, never to return.

Visiting relatives enjoyed the slow pace of Allahabad, after the hectic life of Calcutta. Sleeping under the starts was a luxury long forgotten in the big city and they loved the row of beds in Kanchan Villa's garden on summer nights.

At sunset, Raghu, the mali, sprayed the lawn with water to cool it down. A steam-like haze of heat rose from the ground for the first few minutes, after which the air smelled fresh and inviting. Wicker chairs were placed on the lawn and the evening spent outdoors, entertaining visitors, sipping nimbu pani (fresh lemon drink) and swatting at mosquitoes.

After dinner the wicker chairs were replaced by string cots, complete with bedding and mosquito nets. Matkas of water and tumblers, placed by the beds, quenched nightly thirsts. With the family safely tucked up, the house was locked and the keys firmly placed under Kanchan's pillow.

Sleep being impossible because of the heat, the singing and story-telling went on well into the night. On full-moon nights, the garden was bathed in a silver glow. The heady scent of jasmine and 'Queen of the Night' filled the nostrils and sleep came easily.

Occasionally, a dust storm rudely awakened the sleepers. It whipped off mosquito nets and sent water pots flying. With sand-like dust in eyes and mouths, there was a mad scramble for the house to avoid falling branches or the collapse of the bamboo poles that held up mosquito nets. The only consolation was that a dust-storm usually preceded rain. After a brief spell of rain, the next night was clear and starry and the earth smelled fresh and 'monsoony'. Once the monsoons started in earnest, it was time to move indoors again.

Mango trees shaded the lawn and fruit often fell on mosquito nets during the night. In the morning, Sunny and Anu competed for the most mangoes. Anu always won. It was not until they were older that Purna confessed to rising early to toss fallen mangoes on Anu's mosquito-net.

If there were summer house-guests at Kanchan Villa, beds were made up on the roof terrace as well. Purna's sister, Sulochana Singh, was married to a Sikh gentleman. She bore him four sons, whom she ruled with an iron hand. When she arrived with her son,

Anand, and his new bride, it was decided that the women sleep on the lawn and the men on the roof. During the night, Sulochana heard giggling from within her new daughter-in-law's mosquito net.

'Anand!' she bellowed, in a voice which woke the slumbering women, 'Get back up the stairs!'

The sheepish young man crawled out of his wife's bed and crept upstairs to his own bed.

Sulochana's eldest son, Ajit, was a favourite with his cousin sisters at Allahabad. Being a lot older, he was 'Ajitda' to the girls, who looked upon him more as a brother than cousin. He repaid their adoration by being the only one of his family to maintain contact with them until he died, beloved to the end.

16

MINDING THEIR LANGUAGE

When Sunny progressed to St Joseph's Boys School, Anu and Dolly moved up to St Anne's Convent's secondary section. At four years old, Molly was ready to start school. Purna went along to see the Reverend Mother. Pointing out that he would now have three daughters at St Ann's (as well as a prospective fourth) he felt he was entitled to a concession of some sort. After all, British and Anglo-Indian girls were not required to pay any fees at all. At a time when India was the jewel in Britannia's crown, was it fair that Indians should be second-class citizens in their own country? While Reverend Mother regretted there was no provision for Indian pupils, she had an idea.

'Mr Sarkar,' she said (rhyming it with Parker, rather than the correct 'Sur-kaar'), 'if you were to change your name from Sarker to Parker, we could pass the girls off as British in our records!'

'Mother,' Purna indignantly replied, 'I am proud to be Indian, and I will pay for my daughters' education.'

He stormed out of her office and enrolled Molly – and later Holly – in St Mary's Convent instead. In years to come, Holly's daughter and grand-daughter would attend her alma mater, too.

Around this time, Mahatma Gandhi's 'Satyagrah' movement, or non-violent protest, was rapidly spreading throughout the country.

The program included the boycott of British goods and dress. Allahabad's most famous family was at the fore. Jawaharlal Nehru, educated at Harrow and Cambridge, and his father, Motilal, were thoroughly English gentlemen. Now, their three-piece suits, previously sent to London for cleaning, served as fuel for bonfires of British goods. Jawaharlal's little daughter, Indira, was proud to throw her English dolls on the fire. The Sarkars did their bit – Kanchan stopped buying her daughters' frocks and hats from Whiteway Laidlaw. Apart from this, they had few dealings with British firms.

Since government officers and clerical staff were urged to replace English with Hindi, the far-sighted Purna could see that independence would bring a shift in the official language of the country. India's original tongue, Hindi, would replace Urdu and English, the languages of Moghul and British invaders. Hindi was spoken all around them and even Kanchan was able to speak it fluently, albeit with a strong Bengali accent. But Purna was concerned that his children had very little experience of written Hindi. In a bid to compensate for this failing, he made a radical decision. When Anu was fourteen, he withdrew her and Sunny as well as the thirteen-year-old Dolly, from their schools, to be tutored at home for a year – the accent being on Hindi. The Muslim maulvi, hired to help Sunny and Anu with their Urdu, was replaced by a Hindu pundit. Each weekday, after a morning of Hindi with the pundit, the children had lunch and then resumed studies in other subjects with another tutor. Purna hoped that, after this intensive year, all three children could return to school at the same level as Sunny. It was a huge burden to place on the children.

Eventually all three children returned to school and Anu passed her High School Examination in 1936 from Jagat Taran Girls' School. Sunny passed the exam as well but Dolly, understandably, failed to keep up with the older two, dropping down to a lower class. In the long run, however, both she and Anu gained a year.

The multi-language system was reinforced at home, too. Purna spoke to his children in Hindi, while Kanchan adhered to Bengali. At school and amongst themselves the children spoke English. Purna's foresight paid off when the country was partitioned and official languages determined – Hindi for India and Urdu for Pakistan.

After all the children had finished their exams, the family went to Calcutta on holiday. There, talk among the relatives turned to finding a suitable groom for the sixteen-year-old Anu. Until a likely candidate presented himself, her parents agreed she should continue with her studies.

On their return to Allahabad, Sunny announced he no longer wished to return to education. His parents were dismayed at their only son's decision. Purna mentioned his disappointment to his boss, Sir John Thom. The judge had a solution – he would use his influence to secure Sunny a job in the Civil Secretariat at Lucknow, the state capital. Kanchan wept bitter tears when her firstborn left for Lucknow. Although Purna was relieved that Sunny was appointed PA to the Chief Secretary, his disappointment in his son never left him. He sought compensation in Anu's bright, ambitious and positive nature, relying more and more on her as time went by.

Anu enrolled in Croswaith Girls College to prepare for her Intermediate – pre-university – exams. One of the first girls she met was Shirin Ghilani, a tall and beautiful Afghan girl. When she mentioned the name at home, Purna's ears pricked up. He had just worked on a case involving the wrongful imprisonment of an Afghan called Belti Shah Ghilani. As a result of the trial the man had walked free but Purna refused to divulge the nature of the case to Anu. Belti Shah was, indeed, Shirin's father and Anu correctly guessed he was a political refugee. The unrest along the North West Frontier had driven many Afghan refugees across the border. The tall, bearded men wore large turbans and long shirts over baggy salwars, often in cornflower-blue cotton. In the winter they added colourful embroidered waistcoats to their costume. They traversed the streets on bicycles laden with saddle bags, selling dried fruit and nuts which they imported from Afganistan. Their cry of 'Kabuli wallah!' was familiar all through north India. A handsome and dignified race, they were treated with respect and sympathy wherever they chose to re-settle. Belti Shah Gilani, being of the aristocracy, did not have to resort to the desperate measures of his fellow-Afghan refugees. His daughter, Shirin, and Anu became good friends.

17

THE LOST YEAR

When Anu was preparing to sit her pre-university exams, two maiden doctors, May and Rose, approached Purna to consider 'giving' Anu to their nephew. The Revd John Eric Drummond was chaplain at the church and had noticed Anu as she sang in the choir. The handsome young cleric was secretly fancied by many girls in his congregation and Anu was privy to their giggly confessions. Eric's cousin, Jane Drummond, was Holly's classmate at St Mary's Convent and often visited Kanchan Villa.

Anu was flattered by Eric's approach, via his aunts. Although she had no strong feelings for Eric at the time, she felt she could grow to love him. His maiden aunts' offer was accepted and the engagement went ahead. To match her ring of oval emerald surrounded by twelve diamonds, Anu wore a vibrant green sari embroidered in gold. Her fiancé marked the occasion by giving her an unusual present – a silk parasol which, when opened, revealed a magnificent underside of French lace. In return Anu gave her fiancé a gold signet ring, engraved with his initials and Purna presented him with a suit and gold wristwatch.

Since Eric's aunts felt Anu should be groomed for her future role as a priest's wife, they saw no point in her continuing education. Anu was unhappy at being forced to quit her studies. Her classmates, however, were envious of her. They had drooled over her engagement ring and knew she was preparing for a role they all aspired to. Best of all, she didn't have to study any more. Anu did not share their views. Although pleased that a good match had been found for her, she had hoped to at least complete the academic year before getting married.

Eric visited Anu at Kanchan Villa once a week and they sat in the drawing room, talking quietly, while her younger sisters peeped through the lace curtains, their tittering causing Anu to blush. Prashad carried in the tray of refreshments for the couple, before hurrying back to report snatches of conversation, however mundane, to the younger girls. Eric was ten years older than his bride-to-be but seemed impervious to her nervousness and diffidence. While he did most of the talking, Anu learned very little about his family. She only knew that he had been brought up by aunts May and Rose. After Eric had visited a few times, Anu was allowed to go out with him. He took her to dinner at his maiden aunts' house, where they lectured the nervous sixteen-year-old on wifely duties. It didn't escape the young girl that the two women had never been married.

Kanchan excitedly began to plan Anu's wedding. Jewellery was an important part of an Indian bride's trousseau. Kanchan had set aside her Victorian ruby and pearl suite for Anu when she was carving up her jewellery between her daughters. But there was more to add to this, so a visit to the family jewellers, Ghanshyam Das, was arranged.

Preparing to be a vicar's wife.

Anu fancied a sapphire suite and Purna was on the point of buying it when the jeweller intervened.

'Sapphires are not lucky for everyone, sahib,' he said, 'take a sapphire home and let the Miss Sahib sleep with it under her pillow. If she has pleasant dreams, come back and buy what she has chosen. I will set it aside for her.'

Anu placed the sapphire under her pillow at night but had the most frightening nightmares. She could not wait for morning to tell her parents. Kanchan would not have the unlucky stone in the house for another second – Purna had to take it back to the jeweller immediately. He hailed a tonga and headed for the shop. On the way, the horse bucked, turning the tonga on its side. Purna was hurled into a drain, badly shaken but unhurt. Truly, the sapphire was an unlucky stone. He returned the gem to the jeweller, thanked him for his advice and promised to bring Anu back to make her choice. Anu took her time thinking about it.

Shortly afterwards, Eric was posted to St Thomas's Church in Saharanpur, Anu's birthplace. The young couple corresponded by post, the letters vetted by Purna. When a reliable friend informed Purna that Eric's mother had died of tuberculosis, he was concerned. Now it made sense why Eric never spoke of his mother – he had been too young to remember her – and why his aunts had brought him up. Purna was even more concerned when Eric's letters became few and far between. He consulted Bishop Saunders, the Bishop of

Lucknow, who admitted he had received worrying reports and suggested Purna pay his future son-in-law a visit.

At Saharanpur, Purna sought out the Revd Drummond in his church. Unable to find him, Purna got talking to the verger who, unaware of the stranger's identity, referred to the vicar's 'girlfriend', Sylvia Thomas. A deeply distressed Purna returned to Allahabad. Once again, he consulted the Bishop who advised him to call off the engagement. Wedding plans were cancelled and Prashad travelled to Saharanpur to return the ring and umbrella. Eric was slow to return Anu's letters which, although perfectly innocent, could damage a girl's reputation in the India of 1937. Finally, the Bishop ordered him to return Anu's letters and make an honest woman of Sylvia. (Eric married Sylvia and the couple eventually emigrated to England. Many years later, his cousin Jane told Anu that Eric died of tuberculosis.)

Anu felt her life had been turned upside down. She had been betrayed by a man of the cloth and was unsure of what her future held. At night she quietly sobbed into her pillow, feeling her life had no direction. No marriage. No studies. Now what? Her mother was too busy with the younger children to notice how traumatised Anu was by recent events. Her father, as always, told her to put on a brave face.

'Never let the world see your scars,' he said, providing her with her motto for life.

Taking charge of her life, Anu returned to her studies at Croswaith Girls' College, despondent at being a year behind her peers. She missed her friends, who were now at university, particularly Shirin Ghilani. She may have felt better had she known their paths would cross again, many years later.

In June 1939 Anu passed her Intermediate Exam. The certificate, awarded by the Board of High School and Intermediate Education, United Provinces, listed her subjects as English Literature, History and Allied Geography (Indian British), Economics, Physiology, Hygiene and Elementary Psychology.

Anu was pleased. She felt in control of her life again.

18
ALLAHABAD UNIVERSITY

Anu's proudest moment was when she enrolled as a student in the prestigious Allahabad University, in July 1939.

The institution, established in 1887, started out as an examining body for graduate and post-graduate degrees in classical branches of learning. At the start of the new century, it opened its own teaching departments, while encouraging doctoral research programs. It achieved full status as a unitary teaching and residential university in 1921, a year after Anu's birth.

Allahabad University was a monument to the influences of the city's rich history. It was built in an attractive blend of Victorian and Islamic styles. The sprawling campus housed many buildings and boasted an extensive library. During the freedom struggle, the university became a breeding ground for political activists, producing some of India's greatest leaders and nationalists. (In 2005 both houses of Parliament passed 'The University of Allahabad Act', in recognition of the national importance of the institution.)

Anu felt privileged to enter the portals of such a hallowed institution. She opted to read history, her favourite subject at school, where the girls composed a little ditty to memorise the wives of Henry VIII.

Catherine of Aragon – was a paragon.

Ann Boleyn – longed to be queen

Jane Seymour – a silent schemer

Catherine Howard – was no coward

Ann of Cleeves – wiped with leaves

Catherine Parr – luckiest by far.

Among her fellow-students were her childhood friends, Sammy and Ivy Pratt – whose father worked with Purna in the High Court – and Srirama Mehta, who lived in Lasombe's Field. Her father was editor of the English language daily, 'The Leader'. Srirama's sisters were contemporaries of the younger Sarkar girls. Whilst others had to wait for publication of results in the newspapers, the Mehta girls had an advantage. On the eve of publication, before the paper was put to bed, they wrote little notes to the Sarkar girls, informing them of their results.

Anu threw herself into university life, joining various societies. As a member of the Debating Society, she entered the Inter-University Debate at Ewing Christian College. Anu argued for the motion '*If you want peace, you must prepare for war.*' In the audience, Dolly was more nervous than Anu, as debaters thrust home their arguments. She need not have worried – Anu romped home with the silver medal.

When the Drama Society auditioned for a play, Anu won the role of duchess. Her character was the victim of a burglary, expected to scream, 'My pearls!' on discovery of the theft. Being less than five feet tall with a small voice, projecting her scream to the back of the auditorium was proving difficult. Purna's bank manager came to the rescue. One Sunday, the Englishman opened the bank, and got Anu to scream until he could hear her at the far end of the bank hall. 'My pearls!' resounded through the cavernous building. As a result of this exercise, Anu's natural speaking voice became louder and more authoritative.

Anu cycled the three and a half miles to university and back, her sari accommodated by the design of the lady's bicycle. She rode through the searing heat of summer, the relentless monsoon rain and the crisp winter air. As soon as she returned home, Prashad rushed to take her bicycle from her. Inside the house, Kanchan was ready with food and drink, according to the season – mango fool and cooling lassi (yoghurt drink) after a sweltering cycle ride, or sizzling vegetable pakoras and tamarind chutney after a severe monsoon soaking. If the weather was particularly inclement or political unrest imminent, Purna insisted that Jagannath fetch Anu in his tonga.

One stormy day, as sheets of monsoon rain impaired visibility and thunder claps deafened the ear, a sudden burst of 'fireworks' stopped the horse in its tracks. Clouds of dust rose up before them and the horse appeared agitated. When Jagannath dismounted to investigate, he found a large crater in the road, caused by a falling meteor fragment. Anu was relieved she had not taken her cycle out that day.

Although Anu had a considerable amount of freedom, Purna was still very protective of his daughter. When fellow-student, Madan Gopal Kaul, was canvassing for president of the Students' Union, he called to Kanchan Villa, seeking Anu's vote. Purna answered the door and when the nervous young man asked to see Miss Sarkar, he boomed, 'Which Miss Sarkar? There are three of them here.'

'Lylie Anurani, sir,' mumbled the young man.

'What about?' demanded Purna.

'I am seeking her vote, sir.'

'Are you a politician? Where did you meet my daughter? How did you know where she lives?'

The questions made him so nervous that Madan left without seeing Anu. The next day he warned the male students to seek an appointment with Anu's father if they wished to visit her. She became the butt of more jokes – it was not enough they offered her a match-box to stand on, so she could see the lecturer. Anu, a popular student, took their teasing in good spirit.

By now, the Civil Disobedience Movement had spread to government offices and educational institutions. Disruption was the order of the day. While the Nehru men were in and out of prison, their women were doing their bit to answer Gandhi's call of peaceful non-cooperation. They continued to hold non-violent demonstrations, despite the death of Indira's beloved grandfather, Motilal, and the imprisonment of her father, Jawaharlal, a leading Congressman.

Indira and her mother, Kamala, led protests to Allahabad University, intending to disrupt classes and shut down 'British' institutions. At the Women's Department gates, they urged students to set aside their books and join the campaign for freedom. When pleading failed, they lay down on the ground, forming a human chain across the gates. While some were deterred by this, others stepped over the prostrate bodies and entered the campus. When Anu defied the protesters, she did not know she was stepping over the prone body of her future Prime Minister, Indira Gandhi.

A large group of men was similarly picketing the Men's Department. Anu and her friends had just got to the library when a group of male students rushed past, hotly pursued by baton-wielding police. The men, who had been trying to torch English books in the library, ran towards the Politics Department. While the girls clung to each other and cowered, the police followed the male students into the corridors, raining blows on them. Many were badly injured while others fled to the safety of nearby Alfred Park. The next day dried blood on corridor walls and floors bore witness to the events of that day. The university was temporarily closed and when it re-opened, the freedom-fighters resumed their non-violent struggle.

They encouraged students to withhold fees and many, thinking it their patriotic duty, did so. Among the most vociferous were two sisters whose grandfather was already a leading light in the struggle for freedom. Eventually, the Vice-Chancellor, in an attempt to name and shame, pinned a list of defaulters on the notice board, with threat of expulsion. The two sisters' names were missing – they had been surreptitiously paying their fees, all the while urging others to withhold theirs. Students, who were expelled for non-attendance, were perplexed that the two sisters still remained on the rolls. After all, had they not protested outside the university gates with the Nehru women? It soon became clear that the two girls had been stepping over the protestors' bodies, attending roll call, then stepping over the women again, to join in the daily demonstration at the university gate. Anu, and many of her fellow-students, appreciative of the privilege of attending Allahabad University, had continued to pay their fees and attend lectures. They were sorry, though, to say goodbye to those who were struck off the rolls.

19

WORLD WAR II

1939 was the year when Anu left her girlhood behind and grew into a young woman with family responsibilities. In July, just as she started in Allahabad University, Purna was taken ill. He travelled to Calcutta with Kanchan for surgery, leaving Anu to run the house and care for her younger sisters, while studying for her BA.

The renowned surgeon, Dr Bidhan Chandra Roy, (later Chief Minister of Bengal) successfully removed a large stone from Purna's gall bladder. When they returned from Calcutta, Purna proudly showed off his stone, which he used as a paperweight. Normal life resumed...for a while. The news that Germany had invaded Poland was of no interest to Anu. Little did she realize the implications it would have on her country and family.

In September, World War II broke out in Europe. As in the previous world war, India was dragged into it by her rulers and 600,000 Indian soldiers were sent overseas. The Indian Army grew to more than two million, under the command of both British and Indian officers. Congress politicians, enraged at the use of Indian soldiers as cannon fodder, resigned en masse. The way was cleared for Muslim separatists to step up their campaign for the independent state of Pakistan.

The war panicked the government into scaffolding the Taj Mahal, as protection from German bombings. The monument's white marble dome glowed like an opal, particularly on moonlit nights.

Rumours of war circulated around the bazaars and were brought to Kanchan Villa by the vendors who stopped by the house every day. Purna's barber, too, had his own version and opinion of events. However, the radio offered the best reports, updated as the war progressed. A young reporter, George Orwell, joined the BBC's Eastern Service. His broadcasts of British propaganda were aimed at gaining Indian support for the war. However, Orwell's leanings towards independence for India, caused him to dismiss his time as a broadcaster as 'wasted years.'

The Viceroy, Lord Linlithgow, enjoying the cool respite of the summer capital, Simla, sought 'private advice' from the Governor-General, Lord Gowrie. In an informal letter, he wondered if 'His Majesty's Government in India (which is of course geographically well situated) should be developed as a supplementary base for the whole of this area.'

The shrill sound of air raid sirens became all too familiar. If a siren went off when Anu was cycling back from University, she dropped her bike at the side of the road and lay down. Once, when she was returning home in Jagannath's tonga the scream of sirens caused the horse to rear. Anu and her fellow passengers quickly scrambled off the tonga and lay down on the dusty roadside. Jagannath struggled to get the horse to lie down. In the end, succumbing to the hysteria around him, he lay down beside his passengers, leaving the horse to buck until it overturned the tonga.

Black-out blinds covered windows at night, while local young men patrolled their own areas, checking that no light was visible. Black tin shades covered light bulbs, throwing little pools of light in which Anu and her sisters hunched over their study books. Staples, such as rice, wheat and sugar were rationed. Raghu Bibi sifted the rice and sugar several times to eliminate tiny white pebbles, used to add weight. She sieved the wheat flour, to remove husk which made the flour heavier. The Sarkars grew much of their own fruit and vegetables and Purna's poultry provided sufficient meat and eggs for the table. Except for a few hardships, life continued as normal.

In 1942, Japan invaded Burma and was poised to enter India. Gandhi, believing that British withdrawal would cause Japan to lose interest in India, passed the 'Quit India!' resolution. His peaceful campaigns quickly turned to open rebellion, resulting in the paralysis of national life.

For Anu's parents, there was heartache at the plight of their beloved Bengal. Japanese presence in Burma led to the bombing of Calcutta. In rural Bengal, failing rice crops and epidemic diseases wiped out nearly 3,500,000 people. Thousands of refugees, fleeing famine-stricken villages, filtered into neighbouring states. Some found their way, through Bihar, into United Provinces. The Sarkars were saddened to see groups of famished families, with dejected faces and scrawny children, dragging themselves through Allahabad.

Too proud to beg, they roamed the streets with a drummer at the head of their column. Beating on his dholak he led them in songs of Bengal and her misfortunes.

In the land of rice I see

Not a grain of rice, nor tree.

All around me is the sound

Of teardrops falling on the ground.

The songs deeply moved the Bengali residents of Lukergunj. Kanchan and her neighbours gave the refugees clothes, food and money. Folk were in awe at their ability to sing in the face of such misfortune.

Taking advantage of the turmoil in Calcutta, Kanchan's brother, Nepen, sold the family house without the knowledge of his brothers and rendered their mother homeless. Ostracised by his siblings, he tried to make amends by giving them small amounts of money as their 'shares' – too meagre to buy decent property in Calcutta. His brother, Dhiren, put this money towards a small house, which boasted its own lake, in a village called Thakur Pukur, on the outskirts of Calcutta. He took his mother with him and together they lived a peaceful life, growing their own food. Now, when Didima came to Allahabad, she brought fish from her own lake.

Once, during the monsoons, Kanchan set out to visit her mother. The train was prevented from proceeding beyond a station, as the tracks were submerged under rainwater. The guard herded all the women into the waiting room, where he locked them in for the night to protect them from strange men. The next day, when the trains were running again, he let them out to continue their journey.

As the war raged on, Purna felt a shadow descend on the High Court when Justice Tej Narain Mulla lost his son to the war. Anand Narain was in command of a ship when it was torpedoed. The young officer went down with his crew. Purna's boss, Sir John Thom retired and was succeeded by Sir Trevor Harris. Before long, the role of Chief Justice was taken over by Indian judges.

Rationing was extended to cover kerosene oil, coal and clothes. With Sunny away and Purna retired and unwell, Anu assumed the role of head of the family. She cycled to the ration shop in Karelabagh and queued to receive the family's quota of fabrics – two saris each for Kanchan and herself, and for her sisters, whatever dress fabric was available, be it cotton, voile or parachute nylon. For their undergarments she had to accept 'markin', a cheap, coarse cotton, previously used only by the very poor.

There was more humiliation for the Indian in his own country – the arrival of American soldiers. Flashing their cash, they soon monopolised most services. Now, emerging from the cinema, it was impossible for Purna and his family to hire a tonga or rickshaw. All available transport was commandeered by the GIs and their Anglo-Indian dates – the girls had abandoned British 'tommies' for the free-spending Americans.

Sunny was doing well at the Secretariat in Lucknow and came home to Allahabad once a year. On one such, visit he was amused to find his mother and sisters preoccupied with the latest film at the local cinema – 'Gone with the Wind'. There was so much talk about the dashing Clarke Gable and the feisty Vivian Leigh that Purna agreed they should see it. Not interested in going himself, he put the ladies in Sunny's charge. On arrival at the cinema, the girls were outraged to find that Purna had paid for his wife and son to sit in the expensive box seats. The four girls sat in the cheaper stalls below. It did not ruin their enjoyment of the show, though. Being an unusually long film, it had two intervals, during which they rushed out to buy food and drink from stalls, especially set up in the grounds of the cinema. For days afterwards Kanchan Villa rang with 'Frankly, my dear, I don't give a damn'. Kanchan 'tut tutted' each time the word 'damn' was uttered but admitted she had seen no better film.

20
NEIGHBOURHOOD WATCH

To the left of Kanchan Villa, a high wall separated the Sarkar's house from that of a Muslim family. Khizir Khan worked in the Secretariat and was friendly with Purna. When his boundary wall was under construction, he asked Purna's permission to climb onto Kanchan Villa's roof to check the height of the wall. He did this several times until the wall was high enough to shield his own terrace from the street. This was because his young daughters spent winter days on the terrace, embroidering their colourful Islamic costumes. They sat on a carpet and sewed elaborate patterns with braids, fringes, beads and sequins on their satin gararah suits – long-sleeved tunics over culottes, gathered at the knee. If Sunny or Prashad appeared on Kanchan Villa's terrace, there was a flurry as the girls ducked under the carpet until the man was out of sight.

Occasionally, the Sarkar girls joined them on the terrace and together they sewed the afternoon away. They were so fascinated by the costumes that Kanchan got Kizir Khan's tailor to produce gararah suits for the younger girls. The lilac and green satin outfits were teamed with muslin stoles, or dupattas.

Khizir Khan's wife often visited Kanchan with her youngest daughter, who was blind. Although the toddler was happy to be rocked in Kanchan's arms, her senses were so heightened that she recoiled if Anu or her sisters attempted to touch her.

Molly and Holly in gararah suits

Behind Kanchan Villa, facing the field was a large bungalow, rented by another Muslim family. The white-bearded Shabir Rehman Ghori was Inspector of Schools and a very orthodox man. His Moghul blood was evident from his handsome features and regal bearing. His pretty wife's creamy complexion and blue-grey eyes confirmed her Afghan roots. Their daughter and son-in-law, also a Ghori, lived with them. Unlike his conservative father-in-law, the handsome young man dressed in the style of an English gentleman. The Sarkar girls called the young couple 'apa' – older sister – and 'dulha bhai' – brother-in-law. Their two little daughters, Farida and Walida, spent hours in Kanchan Villa, following Kanchan around. She enjoyed fussing over them, now that her own daughters were grown up. It amused the Sarkars that Ghori Sr. attended his grandchildren's school concerts with cotton wool in his ears so as not to hear the children singing non-Islamic hymns.

Every Sunday, he sent the family on an outing, often accompanied by the Sarkar sisters. Blinds blacked out the car's windows and the driver turned his back while the women boarded. First in was Apa, completely covered in her burqha. Then Anu and her three sisters squashed in beside her, in the back seat. Farida sat on her lap, while her brother, fourteen-year-old Atiq, sat beside the driver. The toddler, Walida, was left in Kanchan's care.

They drove far into the dusty countryside until the driver found an agreeable and shady spot. He parked the car under a tree and then left the ladies to get organised, while he found a large rock behind which to eat his tiffin and have a nap. The women quickly made themselves comfortable on rugs and velvet cushions. They always brought the same food – kebabs, parathas (fried chapatis that peel away in layers) and potatoes mashed with onion, tomato, chilli and coriander. Afterwards, they ate sticky sweet halwa and sipped fruit juices. Apa was happy to feel the fresh air, rid of the purdah for a few hours. She enjoyed the company of the Sarkar girls, laughing and joking with them. Her brother, Atiq, free of his father's control, aimed at birds with his catapult and sang at the top of his voice. At exactly 3 pm the driver called out, Apa donned her burqha and the party packed up and headed home.

Shabir Rehman Ghori was as strict with Atiq as he was with the women in his family. Despite being a child, compared to the Sarkar girls, he was not allowed to mix with them. He watched longingly, from across the fence, when the girls played badminton in their garden. Eventually, with the help of the driver, he found a way to outwit his father. As soon as he spotted his neighbours putting up the badminton net, Atiq jumped over the garden fence and joined them. He played badminton, with his mother's blessing, until his father was due home. The driver tooted the horn as he turned the corner as a warning. In a flash, Atiq jumped the fence and was home just as the car turned into the gate.

The dignified old man's contribution to society was acknowledged when he was named in the King's New Years Honours List in 1937. He was to be conferred with the title 'Khan

Bahadur' by the Governor, Sir Maurice Haig. He invited Purna and Anu to the ceremony at Government House. Anu was thrilled. The only time she'd seen a Governor was some years ago, when Sir Malcolm and Lady Hailey visited Allahabad. Barricades erected in Civil Lines held back crowds, waving Union Jacks to welcome the couple. Now, Anu was pleased to meet Lady Haig and take in the luxurious surroundings of Government House.

A few months later, Khan Bahadur was transferred to another district and the two families lost touch. After Independence, Purna heard the Ghoris had moved to Karachi in Pakistan.

Another Muslim family moved into the Ghoris' house in Lukergunj. Zunnurain rented the house for himself, his sister – again 'apa' to the Sarkar girls – her husband and their daughters. Zunnurain was good-looking, westernized and polished, but his sister was in purdah. He insisted that his nieces attend an English school. Anu knew Zunnurain from University – he was a year ahead of her and their paths often crossed on the campus.

Anu and Dolly often accompanied apa to the cinema – late night show only, when she was less likely to run into women she knew. Zunnurain provided the transport and the Sarkar family got to know him, too. He proved to be a good neighbour the night Purna suffered terrible colic pains. Sunny knocked on Zunnurain's door for help. He immediately drove Sunny to fetch the doctor and, after Purna's pain was relieved, drove the doctor home.

114

Anu was unaware that Zunnurain fancied her. He confessed his feelings for her at a University function but all Anu could do was blush. She was unsure of her own feelings but certain that her father would never countenance his daughter marrying a Muslim and living life in purdah.

21

HALCYON DAYS

Purna and Kanchan built a halcyon's nest for their family, amid the raging wars of Independence and World.

The girls continued their education, Anu and Dolly at University and the two younger girls at St Mary's Convent. While Holly was a bright and eager pupil, Molly showed no interest in her studies. Purna supervised her homework – something he never had to do with the other girls. Kanchan noticed she was spending a lot of time alone on the roof terrace. Fearing she may be depressed, Purna went upstairs to talk to her. He found her signalling to a young man on the terrace of the Pauls' house, at the bottom of the street. When the man spied Purna, he ducked behind the parapet. Molly admitted to secret roof-to-roof communications with Donald Paul. Purna was furious. Don was six years older than Molly. She was only fifteen and still at school, albeit reluctantly. Her parents barred her from going upstairs alone and she sulked indoors for a few days. Then she took to strolling in the garden and hanging about the little wicket leading to the field. Her suspicious father walked round the boundary wall to investigate. He saw Don chatting to Molly as she leaned on the wicket. Creeping up behind him, Purna threw a punch. The young man fled and Molly descended into a sulk again. Keeping a constant eye on her was proving to be a headache.

The problem was solved when Don's father, locally known as 'Old Man Paul', formally called on the Sarkars.

'Don tells me he has fallen in love with Molly and, as far as I know, his feelings are returned,' he told Purna.

'My daughter is only fifteen,' said Purna, 'your son should know better than lead a young girl astray. Tell him to keep away from her.'

Old man Paul had a suggestion, 'Rather than try to keep the young couple apart, why not let them marry?'

The more they thought about it, the more Purna and Kanchan warmed to the idea. The Pauls were Indian Christians and known to the Sarkars – this could be the answer to their prayers. They set about organising the first family wedding. The date they chose was that of their own wedding, 27th of October. The year was 1943.

Anu, conscious of the straightened circumstances imposed by the war, made a decision. Putting her heartache behind her, she handed Molly the entire trousseau from her own failed marriage plans. There was no need to rely on ration cards for the bridal party's clothes either. Molly wore the white and gold silk sari Anu would have worn as a bride. The amethyst chiffon saris that Dolly and Molly were to wear as Anu's bridesmaids were now worn by Dolly and Anu herself, as Molly's bridesmaids. The two flower-girls, Holly and her friend, Beryl 'Mac', wore the same dresses they would have worn as Anu's attendants – lemon organdie dresses with amethyst sashes round the waist.

Old Man Paul owned a pony and trap that was a well-known sight in the area. When he was widowed, his spinster sister, Alice, moved into the family home and brought up his three daughters and two sons. The pony and trap was acquired to take Alice and the girls around Allahabad. Now, for the wartime wedding, the trap was bedecked with flowers from the Paul's garden. The driver and fourteen-year-old 'footman' sported smart sherwanis (Nehru jackets) and turbans with long tails. Clutching her bouquet of garden flowers, the sixteen-year-old bride daintily lifted her wedding sari and boarded the trap. Her proud father sat alongside her and the horse trotted off, the long tail of the footman's turban flying in the breeze. They arrived, to much applause, at the cathedral.

Don and Molly leave the cathedral in the pony trap.

The bridesmaids took their positions behind the bride and as the strains of 'Here Comes the Bride' struck up, Anu felt tears sting her eyes at her own lost dreams. Remembering her father's 'Never let the world see your scars,' she composed herself and slowly followed her younger sister down the aisle.

A reception, in a large 'shamianah' at Kanchan Villa, followed the ceremony. Kanchan had saved rice and wheat from their rations for weeks to provide for the wedding dinner. The rest of the feast was made up by Purna's poultry and vegetables and fruit from Kanchan Villa's gardens. For their part, the Pauls' provided the wedding cake – Old Man Paul's job in the Royal Army Supply Corps office had been useful in getting extra vouchers. The cake was baked by the Muslim baker who produced Christmas cakes for Indian Christians in the area.

During the reception, Aunt Alice found a moment for a quiet word with the bride's mother.

'Kanchan,' she whispered, 'I hope you have explained Molly's marital duties to her.'

Kanchan replied that she hoped Molly's new husband would be as sensitive as Purna, when it came to intimate matters. Alice quickly pointed out that she had brought Don up to be a perfect gentleman. With no more worries, the two 'mothers' rejoined the party.

As celebrations neared the end, Anu helped the bride change

into the pink and gold sari that was meant for her own 'Going Away.' Molly bade a tearful farewell to her family. The fact that she was only going within shouting distance was beside the point – she was 'leaving' her family. The couple boarded the pony and trap for the short journey home. Not only were they waved off by the guests, but some of the younger ones ran alongside them, all the way to the Pauls' house.

The newlyweds honeymooned in Cawnpore, where Don had been at university. A former East India Company garrison town on the Ganges, Cawnpore, with its sister city, Lucknow, was the site of the infamous Indian Mutiny.

The couple stayed with Don's oldest sister, Phyllis, and her family. Don took his new bride to see the Memorial Garden, built to commemorate the 'Bibighar Well Tragedy' of 1857, when 200 British women and children were slaughtered and thrust down the well. A brutal reprisal annihilated the mutineers as well as innocent civilians. The touching epitaph to the victims brought tears to Molly's eyes. Don, aware of Anu's interest in history, took a photo of the Gothic-style memorial for his new sister-in-law.

On Sunday they accompanied Phyllis and her family to All Saints Memorial Church, near the site of the massacre. Preserved in the vestry was a plan of the original entrenchment, while plaques to the British dead adorned the walls of the church. Don heard Molly's beautiful voice for the first time as she sang in the church. After that he often asked her to sing for him. His favourite was 'Danny Boy' which Molly changed to 'Donny Boy' to serenade her husband.

After a week, the newly-married couple returned to Allahabad where Don started work in a friend's fish wholesale business. They rented a house close to both their families and Molly visited Kanchan Villa every day, returning home when Don was due back from work. She missed her closest sister, Holly, and as soon as Holly came home from school, the two girls climbed the mango tree to have giddy conversations. Molly may have been a married woman, but at heart she was still a young girl.

22
UPS AND DOWNS

The war intruded on the Sarkars' peaceful lives one night, when there was a knock at their door. Prashad hastened to answer it.

'Sahib, it's the police,' he told Purna, 'looking for Dolly Miss Sahib.'

Baffled, Purna went to the door. The police were tracking down an army deserter and had intercepted mail addressed to his house. Among the letters were those from Dolly to the man's wife and the police wanted to interview her. Purna explained that while the wife was his daughter's friend, Dolly had absolutely no idea of the man's whereabouts. Nevertheless, the police continued with their line of inquiry until Purna pleaded with Allahabad's Collector not to implicate his innocent daughter. Dolly was advised to distance herself from her friend until the man was found. There was no more contact between the two girls and Dolly hoped her friend would understand. A few weeks later, they heard that the deserter had been found and arrested. In despair, he hanged himself. When Dolly tried to contact his widow, she found the girl had returned to her hometown. The guilt and grief had such an adverse affect on Dolly that Purna decided she needed to get away from it all for a while.

He arranged for Anu and Dolly to attend Summer School – a sort of Bible Camp – in the cool environs of Mussoorie. The journey involved a train to Dehra Dun and then a bus to the hill station.

Purna organised an escort to accompany the girls to the end of the railway line. The train climbed almost 2,300 feet to the town which nestles in the long Doon Valley. With the Ganges to its east and the Jamuna to its west, it was not surprising that the area produced a fine variety of rice – Basmati. At Dehra Dun, the sisters had their first glimpse of the Himalayan foothills, shimmering in the distance. They had left the plains behind! They bade farewell to their escort and boarded the bus for the 22 mile climb to Mussoorie. As the bus meandered up through the Garwal Hills, the girls gasped at the majesty of the snow-capped Himalayas.

They arrived at their destination which, at over 6,000 feet high, runs along a horseshoe-shaped ridge for the best part of ten miles. The hill station was discovered in 1823 by Capt Young, who built a hunting lodge in the pine forest. From these humble beginnings Mussoorie grew into the 'Queen of the Hills.' Like most other hill stations, it was a typical Victorian summer resort, banning 'Indians and dogs' from the main street, The Mall. Anu and Dolly were excited to be where the Nehrus spent their summers. They were aware of Congressman Motilal Nehru's protest at the ban. He insisted on strolling along the Mall – he would rather pay the fine than be barred from a street in his own country. Anu and Dolly were grateful that Indians were now free to walk The Mall.

An Englishwoman, the kindly Miss Kane, ran the Summer School and gave the girls a warm welcome. The sisters quickly settled into a room with three beds. They met their room-mate, Sarah

Raliaram. The girls rose early to attend morning service in the chapel, conducted by Revd Messenger. The prayers ended with the quaintly-worded school anthem:

Youth undaunted, lift up your head,

Though a hope and dream are dead.

Soon a new beacon is burning

Hope is forever returning...

Anu and Dolly were given concessional rates for their stay in return for helping out at the school, so after breakfast they tidied the living and sleeping areas. A condition of acceptance at the school was that each girl brought a skill or talent to share with the others. Anu offered to teach sewing and embroidery while Dolly agreed to teach English and knitting.

Bible classes were held indoors and out, led by Revd Messenger. A part of the day was spent teaching and learning from each other. Miss Kane had organized various activities to fill their free time – symposiums, concerts and trips.

Two or three times a week, the students collected their tiffins from the kitchen and set off to a beauty spot. Once there, they enjoyed the views, sang hymns and ate their picnic, which alternated between 'English' sandwiches of egg, tomato or cucumber and Indian food of chapatti or puri with spicy vegetable. They were always given a piece of fruit, which they thoroughly enjoyed as they did not get apricots, peaches and plums in the plains. The girls walked leisurely along the three miles of the popular promenade,

124

Camel's Back Road; or trekked down to Happy Valley, all the while delighting in the alluring peaks of the distant Himalayas. Sometimes they climbed up a bridle path to a higher vantage point, Gun Hill. It took its name from the canon that was fired at noon every day, for folk to set their clocks. From the height of the hill they had two amazing views – the snowy mountain ranges to the north and the misty and mysterious Doon Valley to the south.

Anu rests on a hillside in Mussoorie.

Their favourite picnic spot was Kempty Falls for which they boarded a rattly old bus, packed with hill folk and tourists. The stunning waterfall gushed down from a height of 4,500 feet, ending in a lake of cold water. The girls ate their tiffins, deafened by the sound of the mighty waterfall. They laughed at urchins splashing about in the cold lake. In between organized activities, the sisters and their friends strolled down The Mall. The main street had a large market at each end but all along its two mile route were little bazaars selling food, souvenirs and knick-knacks. The girls always returned with beads, bangles, rings and fancy little ornaments, hand-made by hill folk.

Most of the summer passed in this way, with new girls welcomed into the school and old ones waved off. Anu was pleased Purna had paid for his daughters to spend the entire two months at the school, rather than just a couple of weeks. Their roommate, Sarah Raliaram, completed her four weeks and prepared to leave. As her departure was very early in the morning, Anu and Dolly hugged her goodbye the night before. When they awoke the next morning, Sarah had gone ... and so had Dolly's smart new sandals. In their place, was a pair of well-worn shoes that had carried Sarah up and down the hills of Mussoorie.

The sisters were happy until Revd Messenger finished his stint at the Summer School and returned to his own parish.

The following morning, when Anu entered the chapel, she caught her breath. In Revd Messenger's place was a young clergyman from Saharanpur – Revd Eric Drummond. Anu fled the chapel, bewildered. Dolly found her sitting on her bed, trembling.

After the sisters had talked for a while, Anu decided it would not be too bad if she only saw him at morning service. Apart from polite 'Good mornings', the couple did not speak. Anu kept away from Bible classes, hoping no one would bring her absence to the attention of Miss Kane. This routine seemed to work well, until Eric decided to accompany the school on picnics. He ruined Anu's enjoyments of the outings. While others laughed and sang, she kept her distance from the group.

Eventually she could maintain her composure no longer and confided in Miss Kane. Shocked as she was, Miss Kane understood perfectly and agreed to let Anu and Dolly leave the school earlier than planned. The sisters travelled back to the plains.

With her summer plans abruptly curtailed, Anu decided to put the remaining weeks to good use. She began a course in first aid with The St John Ambulance Association. On completion she received a certificate which listed:

His Most Gracious Majesty The King

(Sovereign Head and Patron of the Order)

H.R.H. The Duke of Gloucester, K.G., Etc

(Grand Prior of the Order)

President:

His Excellency The Viceroy and Governor-General of India

Chairman, Executive Committee:

Sir Cameron Badenoch, K.C.I.E., C.S.I., I.C.S.

It took all these great men to certify that Miss Lylie Anurani Sarkar was qualified to render 'First Aid to the Injured'.

The summer was not entirely lost, after all.

HISTORICAL FACTS

Halfway through Anu's final B.A. year, her beloved Didima passed away. The family was concerned for the old lady's health after the death of her favourite grand-daughter, Lily. Although they took care to keep the sad news from their mother, she told them she was worried about Lily because her room had suddenly started to smell of lilies. She asked for her grand-daughter all through her last illness and the name 'Lily' was on her dying breath. With all her daughters due to sit exams, Kanchan could not attend her mother's funeral in Bengal. She shed many tears as she went about her daily chores and there was little anyone could do to comfort her.

Upset as she was at losing her grandmother, Anu continued to study for her final exams in the dim pool of a blackout lamp. If there was a power failure, she tried to study by candlelight. If the air raid siren went off, she had to abandon her studies altogether. The day before the first exam, she was distressed to find a cyst on her eyelid – it impaired her sight and oozed a sticky matter. The Examination Board had provision for such emergencies. When Anu arrived, she found a desk and chair had been set up for her on the verandah of the examination hall. Another student, who had just given birth, was allowed to bring her newborn and ayah. She was taken to a secluded area, every time she had to feed the baby. She sat at her desk at the far end of the verandah and shared the special invigilator with Anu.

With no ceiling fans to cool them, the two women tackled their papers in the blazing heat of summer. Anu wrote as best she could, shielding her bad eye with a hand to protect it from dust and light. Every so often, the invigilator produced cotton wool and water for Anu to bathe her sore eye. The women finished long after the other examinees had filed out of the hall.

Despite the setback, Anu did well in her exams and graduated in November 1941. Her parchment scroll bore the University of Allahabad's circular crest of a banyan tree above the Ganges and Jamuna rivers. Its motto read **Quot Rami Tot Arbores** – As Many Branches, So Many Trees. The subjects listed on her scroll were English Literature, Philosophy and History as well as compulsory English.

A further certificate from the Proctor's Office stated, *'She secured a Post-Graduate Merit Scholarship for having stood first in History among the woman candidates of the year (1941).'*

Below it, in the handwriting of the Proctor, MJ Rehman, was the comment, *'She is among the best students of her classes. One of her teachers regards her work as "exceptionally good". She is very intelligent and has an outstanding critical faculty. Her papers to the Historical Association have been well appreciated.'*

At the bottom of the certificate the standard printed lines read, *'She has not taken part in an association of a character subversive of law and order and has not come under its influence so far as to be guilty of acts of indiscipline'.*

A happy student

Anu continued on to do her MA while Dolly, following in her sister's footsteps, enrolled in Allahabad University. By now, most of the girls from Anu's BA days were awaiting marriage, so apart from Anu, there were only two other girls on the History course – Ivy Pratt and Rohini Razdhani. Post-graduate lectures in English, Politics and History were held in the Men's Department. A little gate separated the Women's Department from the Mens'. A peon guarded the gate, opening it to let the girls out to attend lectures and ensuring they were safely back afterwards.

The professors in the History Department of Allahabad University were all eminent historians of the day. The Head of the Department was the cigar-smoking Sir Shefat Ahmed Khan. Students were ushered aside by porters to make way for the great man as he swaggered past, swinging his walking cane. British History students silently filed into the theatre, ten minutes before the lecture began. The peon took the roll call. Barely literate, he could manage the Indian names, but the English names proved a challenge. 'Leeeleee Anurani Sarkar!', 'Same-yule Harr-arse Prate!' (Samuel Horace Pratt) 'Eevee Meeree Prate!' (Ivy Myra Pratt)….

When all had been accounted for, the great Sir Shefat swept into the room, cigar between teeth. He delivered his lecture to a hushed class in a cultured British accent. One day, his students learned he had been appointed Commissioner to South Africa. They were anxious for him, aware of the country's brutal regime, exposed by Mahatma Gandhi. Their fears were well-founded. Sauntering down a street one day, Sir Shefat was shot dead by a single bullet.

Dr Ishwari Prasad lectured in Medieval History. He also had a degree in law and a doctorate in Literature and was later elected Member of the Legislative Council of Uttar Pradesh (formerly United Provinces). Anu specialized in Medieval History and all her life treasured a book by her professor. Entitled 'A New History of India', it contained the inscription *'Dedicated to my students whose appreciation has been my highest reward and whose service has been my most cherished privilege'*.

Anu joined the Post-Graduates' Study Circle in the History Department. Encouraged by the Professor of Modern History, Dr R.P. Tripathi, she presented a paper to the Literary Society on 'Despotism in the 13th and 14th Centuries'. Later it was published in the Study Circle Journal. In his foreword, Dr Tripathi stated the Study Circle placed students and teachers in 'direct and closer intellectual contact.' Anu felt fortunate to be associated with such distinguished educationists.

In 1943 Anu became the first, in both Sarkar and Pandey families, to gain a Master's Degree. She topped in Medieval History and was awarded a scholarship for another two years.

For the convocation ceremony Anu wore a blue chiffon sari with gold border, complimented by delicate, gold filigree jewellery. Mr Fookson, aware that his customer was less than 5 feet tall, had produced the highest pair of heels Anu could manage. The ceremony was a dignified and stately affair.

Afterwards, Purna took her to a studio to have her photo taken in cap and gown. However, Anu chose not to wear the mortar board, preferring instead to simply don her gown and stand by a table, holding the parchment scroll in her hand. Copies of the photo did the rounds of Calcutta for months.

Anu was sad to leave Allahabad University but happy with the glowing references she received from her professors. To Dr Ishwari Prasad, she was *'a bright and accomplished girl with plenty of common sense.'* He continued, *'I always appreciated her intellectual keenness and her desire to acquire accurate knowledge.'* The Professor went on to write fifty books on history and in 1984 was awarded the Padma Bhushan – an Indian civilian decoration, recognizing his distinguished service in the field of Literature and Education.

Dr R.P. Tripathi described her as a *'clever and smart girl. Her expression and command of English are much above the average.'*

The Professor of European and English History, Dr Shanti Swarup Gupta, referred to her as *'an industrious and intelligent student'*. He was particularly impressed *'by her critical faculty and width of outlook'*.

They all wished her every success in whatever she undertook in the future. Anu undertook to continue with her studies.

24

UNIONS AND DIVISIONS

Purna and Kanchan were proud of Anu's achievements but disappointed in Sunny. Running around with Anglo-Indian girls in the clubs of Lucknow was not how his parents envisaged his future. They decided it was time to consider 'settling' Sunny. Relatives in Calcutta were alerted to the hunt for a suitable bride. Kanchan's sister, Sneh Lata Biswas, readily offered her nubile daughter. As it was legal for cousins on the mother's side to marry, Purna agreed to consider the match. Kanchan and Sunny travelled to Calcutta and all the relatives gathered round to watch the developments. Among them was cousin Onko who had been touted as the 'Pandey family's first graduate' – until Anu surpassed him as the 'Pandey family's first Post-Graduate'. When they retired for the night, Sunny confided in his mother that he suspected his future bride's heart had already been taken by the swaggering Onko. The next morning histrionics and tears abounded as the couple was forced to reveal their secret liaison. Kanchan and Sunny returned to Allahabad, leaving Sneh Lata to arrange a marriage between her daughter and Onko instead.

Then Kanchan remembered her friend, Dilli Bowdi ('Delhi sister-in-law') and inquired if her grand-daughter was ready for marriage. Jyoti Moyee Dey was, indeed, poised on the threshold of matrimony. Once again, mother and son went on a 'viewing' trip –

this time to Delhi.

The meeting proved successful and, two months later, the whole Sarkar family travelled to Delhi for the wedding. They stayed in a wing of the large house owned by Dilli Bowdi. Sunny and Jyoti were married in St John's Church, Fatehpuri, by the Bishop, the bride's godfather. Afterwards, the wedding guests returned to Dilli Bowdi's house. The flat roof terrace was cleaned and 'durries' laid out for a traditional Bengali wedding feast. Like Purna and Kanchan's wedding, guests sat cross-legged on the 'durries' and ate off banana leaves.

A room in Dilli Bowdi's house had been set aside as the bridal chamber. Strings of tinsel, roses and jasmine curtained the four-poster bed. Once the groom had entered the room, the custom was for the blushing bride to be escorted to her new husband by single women guests. A little innocent teasing would follow before the girls left the couple alone. Jyoti's giggling and tittering friends, as well as her new sisters-in-law, walked her to the bedroom door. They were astounded when the bride dismissed them with a wave of her hand and boldly entered the room, shutting the door behind her. The brazen hussy!

When the Sarkars returned to Allahabad with the new member of their family, a reception was held at Kanchan Villa. Having no family accommodation in Lucknow, Sunny left his new bride with his family and returned to his job, making frequent trips back to see his wife.

Sunny and Jyoti.

Inspired by Sunny's wedding, Kanchan's friend, Mrs Gupta, decided it was time to find a bride for her firstborn. Mrs. Gupta was married to a vet and they lived in the neighbourhood with their two sons, Montu and Jhoonu – who later became the Sarkar's family doctor. A local girl, Khushi (Happy) was 'sourced' and Montu's marriage arranged. As was usual at Hindu weddings, a room was dedicated to the display of the dowry the bride had brought with her – brass and steel cooking vessels, silk and embroidered garments, fine bone china and all the modern gadgets of the day. But guests were surprised at the lack of jewellery. Surely the Guptas had not accepted Khushi without the obligatory gold? Their curiosity was satisfied at the ceremony. As the couple settled down beside the sacred fire, the pundit announced that he was now going to weigh the gold Khushi had brought in her dowry. He weighed the jewellery on silver scales before the guests and asked Mrs. Gupta if she was happy with the weight. When she nodded, the guests applauded and the colour came back into Khushi's father's face.

Personal joys continued to be tinged with sadness at national level. The Viceroy, Lord Wavell's efforts to find common ground between Hindus and Muslims was proving unsuccessful. The Muslim League's leader, Mohammed Ali Jinnah, was pushing for a separate state. The patriotic song, Bande Matram, sung for years as an anthem of India, was now viewed as pro-Hindu. Dreams of a united independent India were rapidly fading, confirmed by the ditty:

'A Parsi, a Jew, a Christian or two,

'But Mohammed Ali Jinnah says

"No Hindu"!'

25
A TEACHING CURVE

Armed with her post-graduate degree and glowing references, Anu applied to the Department of Public Instruction, United Provinces, for a place on the Licentiate in Teaching course. She joined the Government Training College, Allahabad, and began her Teachers' Training. Alongside the main course, she opted for specializations in three further subjects – History and, for a change, Crafts and House Crafts.

Inspired by her Principal, the esteemed educationist, Dr Ibadur Rehman Khan, Anu threw herself into college activities. At the annual Sports Day she won positions in several races – her favourite being the 220 yards cycle race. Although an experienced cyclist she still found it hard to pedal as slowly as possible, without falling off. Nevertheless she wobbled into second place on her hardy bicycle.

During the long summer holidays, Molly, now pregnant, came daily to Kanchan Villa to 'play' with Holly – her favourite sister. One day, sitting up in a mango tree, the two girls were alarmed to find water trickling down Molly's legs. Holly scrambled down the tree as fast as she could to tell their mother, who immediately ordered Molly from the tree and made her lie down. Prashad's father was cutting grass when Kanchan called him. He cycled furiously to Dr Hayes' clinic to inform her that 'Molly Miss Sahib's waters had broken'. The American doctor arrived and, deciding the patient had a long labour ahead of her, made herself comfortable on the spacious Victorian double-bed and dozed off. A short while into her nap, she was woken by cries of 'Baby! Baby!' Leaping out of bed she held out her bare hands, in time to catch a baby boy.

'Oooooh', she cooed, 'ain't he just dinky?' And so, unwittingly, she gave the baby his pet-name, Dinky, although he was christened 'Suchet' Desmond.

The baby became the centre of the universe for his grandparents and aunts. Molly, always good at sport, decided to take up badminton again and was happy to leave her baby with her adoring family while she competed in tournaments around the city. As a toddler, he was often found on the knee of an aunt while she studied at her desk. Anu taught him the alphabet and nursery rhymes, which he would proudly recite when Grandpa Paul visited.

While Anu knew her own mind and was determined to continue with her studies, Dolly, although a conscientious student, was shy and reclusive. Kanchan suggested to Purna that they put out feelers for a suitable groom for her. Scouring the Matrimonial Column of The Leader, Purna spotted the perfect 'Bride Wanted' ad. An Indian Christian doctor was seeking a bride from a 'good' family. He was duly contacted and invited to tea to meet Dolly. Sunny, home on leave, teased his sister so mercilessly all day that, by the time Dr. Prim arrived, Dolly refused to come out of her room.

Kanchan with her first grandchild, Dinky

Excuses were made, Dr Prim left and Sunny got the dressing down of his life. Dolly continued at university, pursuing a Master's Degree in English.

1945 was proving to be a year of celebrations. Anu finished her first year of training and was awarded a certificate for specialization in History. Close on her heels, Dolly completed her Masters and, at her graduation ceremony, was announced the winner of the gold medal for English. Again, following Anu's lead, she enrolled for the L.T. course.

The greatest cause for celebration was the end of World War II. The country went mad with excitement. Fairy lights festooned public buildings and people spilled onto the streets to admire the illuminations. Purna hired Jagannath to take the family around the city in his tonga. They rode from one area to the next, all night long, awed by the decorations. The extravagant display of lighting was in sharp contrast to the black-outs of recent years.

The Red Cross organized a massive mela to celebrate the end of hostilities. Thousands converged on the fair grounds and with no more rationing, food stalls abounded. Sunny, home for the public holiday, joined his family and childhood friends at the fair. Suddenly he heard the loud speaker blaring out – 'Lylie Anurani Sarkar to the Treasure Hunt stall please!' He sought his sister out and together they ran to the stall. Anu had placed a pin at the exact spot on a map where the treasure was buried. She was thrilled to win a silver cigarette box, obviously for ladies as it was engraved with roses.

She treasured her prize for life. It lay in her jewellery drawer and was produced with a flourish every time the word prize was mentioned, in whatever context.

26

BASIC TRAINING

After her Licentiate in Teaching and three specializations Anu turned her attention to the concept of Basic Training. In response to Mahatma Gandhi's call for the extension of literacy and basic education to villages, Basic Training Colleges had sprung up all over the country. Anu was introduced to the scheme by her principal, Dr Ibadur Rehman Khan, who also headed the Basic Training College. In addition, the respected academic served as Joint Director of Education.

Anu joined the Basic Training College in Allahabad and worked in the area of Nursery Education. In order to make learning simple for the masses she and her colleagues devised a project called 'Postage Stamp'. A make-believe Post Office was set up in the class-room. The teachers used this base to introduce their young pupils to different subjects. Under Arithmetic, the children learned to buy and sell stamps; under History, they heard the story of Rowland Hill and his penny post; under Geography, the children traced the routes of letters on a map of the world; under English, they learned to write letters; under Art, they designed postage stamps; under Craft, the youngsters made cardboard pillar boxes and dotted them round the playground; and finally, under Drama, the pupils dressed as postmen, delivered letters around the college.

While training at the college, Anu, a keen knitter, produced a little blue sweater for Dr Khan's toddler son, Sabu. The child's mother was so impressed she sought knitting lessons from Anu and the two women became friends. She often asked Anu to help the two older children, Fasim and Naazish, with their studies. Respectfully referred to as 'Begum Sahiba', the lecturer's wife was also in education. She was chairwoman of Hamidia Girls' School – an Islamic school that taught through the medium of English. Begum Sahiba was openly in favour of the partition of India and the creation of the separate state of Pakistan. This was in conflict with her husband's stance on the subject – he was already well-established and highly respected in India.

When Dr Khan was asked to open a new Basic Training College in the state capital, Lucknow, he decided to form a team of his best students to help him set it up. The Public Service Commission began to interview likely candidates. Ivy Pratt's proud father told Purna that his daughter had been singled out for interview. Purna was quick to inform him that Anu, too, had been 'singled out'. When the boiling hot day of the interview arrived, Anu's father sent her in Jagannath's tonga, so she did not arrive on her bike, in a sari wringing with perspiration. Ivy, dressing sensibly for the weather, arrived on her bicycle, in a cotton dress and pith helmet (more popularly known as a 'solar topi' and associated with 'mad dogs and Englishmen'). Unfortunately, her choice of dress was not considered suitable for Gandhi's village scheme.

At the end of the interviews, seven applicants were accepted – six men and one woman – Anu. While Purna was proud of his daughter's achievement, his main worry was for her safety and well-being in Lucknow. There being no provision for 'safe' accommodation, such as the trusted Young Women's Christian Association (YWCA), Purna persuaded Anu to decline Dr Khan's offer. Anu was disappointed, but understood her father's concern.

As a second option, she accepted Begum Sahiba's offer of a teaching post in Hamidia Girls' School. Anu was glad of the job but sad to see the Khans leave for Lucknow. A short time after that, Dr Khan returned to Allahabad to chair a conference. When his photo appeared in 'Sunday Leader', Anu cut it out and saved the treasured snippet in her Bible. (Some sixty years later her daughter took the yellowed cutting to a Dublin stationer to be laminated. The young salesgirl expressed astonishment at the date of the newspaper – April 21, 1946. 'I don't think even me granda was alive then!' she exclaimed.)

After Independence, Anu heard that Dr Khan had succumbed to his wife's insistence and emigrated to Pakistan.

Having studied in Christian schools all her life, Anu found teaching in Hamidia Girls' School a new experience. Although a Muslim school, the majority of teachers were Christian, because the medium of instruction was English. At morning assembly, the girls recited a text from the Koran but it was noticed that some folded their hands in prayer as Christians do. This was quickly put right by the principal. One morning, she pointed out to the pupils that the correct gesture was to place hands side-by-side, with palms upturned – the Muslim way.

World War II may have ended but India's struggle for freedom continued. The Muslim League's support of the war had won them concessions. Whereas before, loud music and blowing of conch shells accompanied Hindu religious processions through streets, now the 'Music before Mosques Ban' applied when Muslims were at prayer and during the forty day period of Ramzan. With the widening of the gap between Hindus and Muslims, partition of the country looked increasingly likely.

Realising the possibility of opportunities in a new country, Molly's husband, Don, decided to move north-west. He reasoned that the first-come-first-served position would benefit him, should he be in Pakistan after partition. Bidding goodbye to Molly and Dinky, and gratefully accepting Anu's first salary, he set off for the western state of Rajasthan. There, he mounted a camel and crossed the Thar Desert to Karachi. Having nowhere to stay, he slept on the beach at night and spent the day looking for work. Eventually he acquired a kiosk from which he sold newspapers. Continuing to sleep on the beach, he saved his money in the hope of renting a house and bringing his family to live with him.

Purna and Dinky off to the market

27

HIGHLAND FLING

By now, Purna had retired and taken to gentle 'retiree' activities. After an early morning shave by the barber, he read 'The Leader', stretched out on his planter's chair. Then he walked to the market, stopping by Molly's house to pick up his grandson. Holding the toddler's hand, he strolled through the market, buying foods that didn't come to the door. He bought bright orange 'jalebis' (syrupy sweetmeats) for Dinky which the child ate from the leaf bowl, sticky syrup running down his little arms.

After lunch, Purna passed his time supervising the mali in the management of fruit trees or fussing over his ever-growing flock of poultry. His hens included red Rhode Islands, black Minorcas, grey Orpingtons and white Leghorns. He also had a cock-bird, ducks and geese. He had recently acquired a turkey, with an aversion to saris. An angry turkey in hot pursuit of sari-wearers became a common sight in Kanchan Villa. No amount of pleading by Kanchan or threats by Raghu Bibi could persuade Purna to get rid of his beloved bird. It was enough that Prashad held the spluttering and fluttering bird back to allow the women to pass.

When Purna noticed he was getting increasingly short of breath, he decided to quit smoking. Throughout their married life Kanchan rolled his cigarettes, placing ten at a time in a silver cigarette case. Purna threw away the purse of 'Old Rip' tobacco and book of cigarette papers and never smoked again.

Kanchan spent her day pottering about the house and supervising the cooking. The high spot of her day was seeing her grandson. Dinky spent more and more time at Kanchan Villa while his mother, having progressed to state champion, travelled all over the province to badminton tournaments. When Sunny's wife, Jyoti, gave birth to their first baby, Dinky acquired a cousin and playmate. Sunny continued to work in Lucknow but made frequent trips to Allahabad to see his wife and daughter, Putul (doll). Eventually, he found family accommodation and took his family away to Lucknow.

When academic institutions closed for the summer, Purna decided to reward Anu and Dolly for their academic achievements, with a reprieve from the intense heat of the plains. But where should he send them?

The answer was provided by Mrs Rufus, from the 'Nawab Sahib's Compound'. Her sister, Kamala, was married to a Goan, who rejoiced in the name Appolian Menzies. He was leader of a jazz band that played for the summer season in the prestigious Boat Club of Naini Tal.

'Kamala wants to join Appolian but is nervous of being left alone while he works halfway into the night,' Mrs. Rufus told Kanchan, 'why not allow Anu and Dolly to accompany her to Naini Tal?'

Purna immediately agreed to the suggestion, delighted that his daughters would be well chaperoned. The two girls packed their trunks and left for the hill station with Kamala 'mashi' (auntie).

The women first travelled by train, overnight to Kathgodam – the end of the railway line – 22 miles south of their destination. Arriving at Kathgodam the following morning, they gazed in wonder at the pine forests around them. The town derived its name from the pine logs it stored – kath (wood) godam (godown). Then they boarded a crowded bus, which snaked its way up the steep and winding tracks of the Kumaon Hills. After driving up to a height of 6,000 ft the tired old bus arrived at the summer capital of United Provinces. The hill station, built around a lake or 'tal', was discovered in 1840 by a sugar merchant called Barron. Some forty years later, a major landslide brought down the Assembly Hall (State Legislature) and the fashionable Victoria Hotel. The debris settled in the valley, creating the The Flats – a recreation area by the lake. The Naini Tal Boat Club stood on the edge of the lake. It was once so exclusive that it refused membership to the area's most famous son, the hunter Jim Corbett, because he was born in India – only 'pukka sahibs' were allowed in.

Kamala mashi and her young companions engaged two coolies, or 'dhotiyals', to carry their luggage up the hill to the house rented by Appolian for the summer. During the day, while the band practiced, the ladies descended the hill, pausing to admire blue and mauve hydrangea and bright pink rhododendrons along the way. They had never seen these flowers in the plains. Down through the rustling trees they made their way to The Flats, mingling with other holiday-makers and taking in the sights. They had a moment of silence at Naini Devi temple, north of the lake, built to honour Lord Shiva's wife, Sati. Her emerald green eye, or naina, was said to form the lake and give the hill station its name. In the evening, they strolled along The Mall to one of the two bazaars flanking the lake – Mallital (head of lake) to the north or Tallital (foot of lake) to the south. There, they spent hours browsing in the shops and eating as much 'hill fruit' as they could – apricots, peaches and plums reminded them of Mussoorie. A three mile walk up from Mallital led to the highest point in the area, Naini Peak, also known as China peak. The women often trekked up at dawn to get a clear view of the snow-capped Himalayas, opalescent in the morning light.

West of the tal, a shorter walk brought them to the tourist attraction, Dorothy's Seat – a viewing point built in memory of the victim of a plane crash. Exhausted from the steep climb, the women were amused to find a local had managed to carry up enough tea-making equipment to set up a stall. They were grateful for a refreshing cup of tea before starting their descent. Often, if tired, or just for fun, they hired a dandy – the three of them squashed into the sedan chair carried by two strong men.

On Sundays, accompanied by Appolian and his band members, they attended morning service at St John's Church. Built in 1847, the churchyard contained graves of the few victims who were dragged from the landslide, while inside, others were remembered on a brass memorial plaque.

Dolly outside the Boat Club in Naini Tal

After two months, when the 'season' was over, Appolian and his band members stayed behind to pack their musical equipment, while the ladies began their return journey to the plains. At Katgodam they boarded the train for Allahabad.

From the far end of the congested carriage, they heard someone call, 'Lylie!' Anu's friends always called her by her English name. She looked up to see a fellow-student from the Politics course at Allahabad University. Gyan Mittal dragged his trunk closer to the girls, sat on it and chatted to them all the way. He was happy to run out at stations to buy their refreshments and newspapers. He told Anu he had joined the army during the war and was a captain, stationed at Allahabad Fort. He was returning from a camp course in Almora, close to Naini Tal and going on to his hometown of Aligarh for a break.

When the girls disembarked at Allahabad, he bade them farewell and promised to contact them on his return to the fort. Little did Anu realize the profound affect his promise would have on her future.

28
YOUNG OFFICERS

Molly, now a 'respectable married woman', was flattered to be her sisters' chaperone when they went out without their parents. One cold December afternoon, she escorted Anu and Dolly to the matinee of 'Gaslight', starring Bette Davis. Settling into their box seats they were approached by two young men in army uniform – Anu's friend, Gyan (who had travelled back from Naini Tal with Anu and Dolly), and his fellow-officer. The friend produced a packet of Vicks lozenges from his pocket and offered it to the girls, which amused them. After the film, Gyan promised to contact them again.

True to his word, he called to Kanchan Villa, accompanied by an English officer, Major Stanley Boucher. Before Purna could 'interview' the gentlemen, Gyan quickly produced a gilt-edged invitation to a party in honour of General Cariappa, in the Officers' Mess at Allahabad Fort. He wished to invite Anu and her sisters. Their old-fashioned father agreed, on condition they were chaperoned by Molly and home by 10 pm. The sisters were excited at the thought of going to their first big army reception. They were also secretly pleased that Gyan had out-witted their father. They had seen the fort's massive walls and high battlements on the Jamuna side of Sangam often enough. Soon they would be privy to its mysterious interior.

Built by the Moghul Emperor Akbar in 1583, the impressive citadel now housed the army. Anu, given her interest in history, was particularly thrilled at the thought of seeing the famed Ashoka Pillar. Dating from 232 BC, it was inscribed with the Buddhist emperor's edicts. Entering the hallowed grounds of the fort filled the sisters with awe.

On the night of the party, the girls dressed with care and after passing their mother's critical eye, boarded the army jeep for the long drive to the fort, escorted by Gyan.

At a party in the fort – Molly, Anu, a friend and Holly

On arrival, he shepherded them through the fort's security posts to the Ordnance Officers' Mess. Inside, the ladies sipped fresh fruit juices while the men knocked back 'chotas' (spirits). The girls had never been exposed to alcohol before and were amazed at the big part it played in army functions. General Cariappa was charmed by Molly who enjoyed his attention, secure in the knowledge that she was safely married. (On Independence, when General Cariappa was appointed the first Indian Chief of Staff, Molly would boast that she had danced with him.) Shy Dolly hovered by Gyan's side all evening, intimidated by the sophisticated surroundings. And Anu...well, Anu caught the eye of a dashing young Ordnance officer, Captain Rameshwar Dutt Vasisht – the Vicks lozenge man. Now, they laughed at their first meeting and the sisters enjoyed themselves so much they lost track of time. It was 2 pm before Gyan brought them home, sneaking off as soon as Kanchan opened the door. The next morning Anu and Dolly were severely reprimanded by their father. They thought it very unfair that Molly, dropped off at her own home, escaped Purna's tirade.

The girls were members of The Three Arts Club, which promoted Indian art and culture. When Anu was elected secretary, Purna was impressed that his daughter had her own calling cards. She enthusiastically led the committee in organizing the club's annual social. They erected a shamianah and ordered food. Alongside Indian samosas, pakoras, and Allahabad's speciality, 'dilbahar' ('happy heart' – a heart-shaped sweet covered in cream),

157

were English delights – meat patties, iced cakes and éclairs. By early evening, to the organisers' dismay, a storm began to brew. The shamianah swayed, cups and saucers rattled and rain lashed down in torrents. The organizers tried to salvage as much food as they could, before the shamianah came crashing down. They divided the food out amongst themselves and went home. With more fancy food than they could consume, Anu organized a party the next evening. She invited their neighbours, including Zunnurain, while Molly sent a messenger to the fort asking Gyan, Stan Boucher and Ramesh to the party. Anu's heart fluttered at the thought of seeing Ramesh again. But only Gyan and Stan Boucher turned up. Ramesh was on Orderly Duty and unable to leave the fort. Anu lost interest in the party but went through the motions of being a good hostess. Zunnurain, still carrying a torch for Anu, sensed her unhappiness and watched her closely. Food was being regularly heated in the kitchen and served to guests in the drawing room. Late in the evening, on a trip to the kitchen for fresh supplies, Anu's heart skipped a beat. Sitting under the jackfruit tree, scraping mud from his heavy army boots was Ramesh. As soon as his duty was over, he had ridden his motorbike as fast as he could to Kanchan Villa. Anu was overjoyed. It suddenly dawned on her that she had fallen in love. Zunnurain, too, realized she had given her heart to someone else. He quietly slipped away from the party.

Gyan introduced his friend to Purna and Kanchan and they took a liking to the tall, good-looking Punjabi officer. The two men visited a few times before suggesting the Sarkar girls join them on a picnic. Purna insisted that Kanchan chaperone their daughters, as Molly was away at a badminton tournament. Another university friend had a mansion overlooking the rivers and Gyan was sure they could request use of the grounds for a picnic. Shyam Nath Kakkar was only too happy to welcome them to Rambagh.

On the appointed day, the two young officers arrived in an army truck, helped the ladies aboard and drove to Rambagh. After enjoying their picnic of puri and kebab, Anu wished to collect shells from the dry bed of the river. Ramesh quickly offered to accompany her and while the two walked bare-footed on the sand, Ramesh professed his love for Anu. She shyly replied that she, too, was growing fond of him. That night, Anu confided her feelings for Ramesh to her mother. Kanchan, in her own gentle way, persuaded Purna to allow the young officer to court their daughter. But they both had reservations. For a start Ramesh was Hindu, and a Brahman the highest caste, to boot. He probably came from an extremely orthodox family, impervious to the influences of their British rulers. Anu's Christian upbringing, on the other hand, had been fairly liberal. They reasoned that his military training had westernised him sufficiently to have some common ground with their daughter. And so, remembering the Eric Drummond fiasco and conscious that their daughter knew her own mind, the couple agreed to allow her suitor to visit.

159

Ramesh was stationed at the Ordnance Depot in Cheoki, an army base on the edge of the city. As soon as he finished work at 6 pm, he mounted his motorbike and, still in his uniform, set off for the hour-long ride to Lukergunj. Around 7 pm, Anu heard the motorbike as it turned the corner to her house and ran out to the gate to greet him. They conducted their courtship on a settee on the chabutra, in full view of everyone. No one was going to give Purna's daughters a bad reputation. Thankfully, their hushed conversations were out of earshot.

Occasionally, they went on outings accompanied by sisters and friends. One such trip was a picnic at Jhusi. Originally the ancient city of Pratisthanpur, this ruin of a town was now just a collection of small ashrams and temples on the sandy banks of the river, where people sought spiritual peace. They held their picnic on an island in the river called 'Sujawan Devta'. A channel of river divided the island in two.

Arriving at their destination by boat, the sisters removed their sandals, hitched up their saris and waded into the channel. In a playful mood Ramesh threw Anu's sandals across the water onto a far sandbank. He would only retrieve the sandals if Anu rode piggyback as he swam out to the sandbank. On their return they found Gyan and Stan chasing Anu's sisters, playing catch. Dolly ran ahead on to a stretch of wet sand. Suddenly, she cried out in horror as the marshy land slowly began to swallow her. When Molly and Holly went to her aid, they too, began to slowly sink into the marsh.

The rest of the party was panic-stricken. Their hopes were raised when a villager passed by with a heavy walking stick.

Anu called to him, 'Baba! Please lend us your stick to help the girls out!'

'And what if my stick is lost in the sinking sand?' he shouted back.

However, he did offer them valuable advice. If they stopped struggling and lay back on the sand, the marsh would offer them up. The three stricken girls held hands and tried to lie back. The men grasped the clothes of the nearest one and used all their strength to pull the chain of girls out. The relieved party rowed back to the jeep and drove to the Officers' Mess at Cheoki. The girls washed themselves in the toilets and, wrapped in towels provided by the men, waited behind closed doors. The young officers laundered their sand-laden saris, hung them before the fire-place to dry and ordered food from the mess kitchen. Anu, the only one who was dressed, liaised between the officers and her sisters. Still trembling from their frightening experience, they hungrily devoured the tea and piping hot pakoras. By 7 pm, they were dressed again and found the men in the bar, calming their nerves with brandies. Although expected home at 5 pm, they did not return until 9 that night. The officers left them at the gate and drove off, afraid to face Purna's wrath. The girls lied to their father that the jeep's punctured tyre had caused the delay. When Kanchan came to kiss them goodnight, she said Purna had threatened to report the officers to their Commanding Officer, had the girls not returned by 10 pm. Safe in their beds, the sisters all agreed that it would have been much worse if four of them had left that morning and only one had returned at night, whatever the time.

The men made themselves scarce for a while. Eventually Stan Boucher called and spun Purna a long yarn as to why the officers had not visited. He asked if he could take the girls to a matinee in the local cinema. Instead, they all met up at a park and went over the whole harrowing experience. The young men had been shaken by it, too.

When Anu and Ramesh went out in a group, the others maintained a discreet distance to allow the couple privacy. They talked about each others' religious traditions as well as that of the army. Although Ramesh's regiment, 'Royal Indian Army Ordnance Corps', could trace its roots back to the 15th century, it had not allowed Indians into the officers' ranks until 1927. Ramesh told her how, on a route march, their British sergeant-major had singled out Brahman cadets and ordered them to wade through an open sewer. He had laughed at the power he had, not just over Hindus but over the highest caste. On their return to barracks, Ramesh had removed the sacred thread worn across a Brahman's torso. What was the point? His caste had been 'spoiled'. He now lived an army life, rather than a Hindu life, aspiring for a country free of the British. He would not have long to wait.

In March 1947 Lord Louis Mountbatten assumed office as the British Governor-General. It looked like he would be the last Viceroy to represent His Majesty's Government in India. Despite opposition by Gandhi to the partition of India, the new Viceroy announced his plan for the division of the country. Predominantly Muslim districts would form the new state of Pakistan while the remainder would comprise independent India. The horrors of partition that lay ahead were not envisaged by anyone.

For the present, Anu was in love and her country was poised on the verge of freedom. Life could not be better.

29

ROMANCE AND INDEPENDENCE

At midnight on August 14-15 1947, India was declared independent and the new state of Pakistan born. All over the country, Union Jacks were lowered and replaced by the Indian tricolour. Church bells pealed, car horns tooted and train whistles blew all through the night, as throngs filled the streets to celebrate. Fireworks emblazoned the skies. Nature seemed to join in the celebrations too as, despite being the monsoon season, the rains held off. In Delhi, India's first Prime Minister, Pundit Jawaharlal Nehru, made his celebrated 'Tryst with Destiny' speech. He hoisted the saffron, white and green flag on the historic Red Fort to jubilant cries of Jai Hind! (Victory to India!)

Sadly, this momentous occasion was marred by the communal riots following partition. Hindus and Sikhs abandoned their homes in Pakistan to cross the border into India, while Muslims fled in the opposite direction. Along the way, they slaughtered and maimed each other, using whatever weapons came to hand – swords, knives, guns and truncheons. Properties were set alight and bloodbaths greeted trains as they carried passengers across borders. 15 million people were rendered homeless. The states of Punjab and Bengal were split into two – one half for each country. This worked well for Punjab, which straddled the border. But it posed a huge problem for Bengal in the east. Pakistan's portion of the state was

600 miles across India. This far-flung limb was named East Pakistan. (Less than thirty years later, it would break away to form the independent country of Bangladesh.) The displacement of Sikhs from the divided Punjab led to violent clashes between Sikhs and Muslims in both countries.

Allahabad was no exception. The Sarkars were horrified to hear that their Muslim baker's five-year-old son had been impaled on a Sikh's sword while the baker himself was rendered blind by another rioter. For days, Kanchan was without help in the house as the servants were too afraid to venture out. Blood-curdling screams rent the air. Hospitals locked their doors to protect patients, as rioting crowds rampaged through the streets. While security forces guarded vital services and buildings, ordinary folk felt defenceless. The District Magistrate recommended that young men group under the leadership of a policeman or soldier to protect their own localities. These vigilante groups patrolled the streets amid heart-rending cries of 'Help me!' or 'Save me!' In the midst of all this hatred there were stories of Hindus protecting their Muslim friends and vice versa. More often than not, they paid the ultimate price for their loyalty.

One man's misfortune is another man's gain. Karachi, where Molly's husband had gone to seek his fortune, was now in Pakistan. As Hindus and Sikhs abandoned their homes and businesses and rushed across the new border to India, Don used his paltry savings to buy a small printing press from its fleeing owner. He occupied an abandoned house and sent for his family. Recalling the earlier arrangement he had made with his father, he sent a telegram with the terse message, 'Meet Atari'. Old Man Paul's return telegram asked, 'Who is Atari. How will I know him?' This exchange became a family joke as Atari was the border town where the old man was to hand Molly and Dinky over to Don. Travel arrangements were made and Dinky's grandparents and aunts were heart-broken when the little boy and his mother left for Pakistan.

Despite the unrest in the city, Ramesh continued to undertake the journey across town to visit Anu. She noted that after Independence the crowns on his epaulets were replaced by the Ashoka Lions of free India. Posts vacated by British officers returning to England were filled by Indians. Ramesh was appointed Liaison Officer for the Ordnance Corps.

By the end of the year, the violence had largely died down. The Sarkars invited Ramesh to join them on Christmas Day, to give him a taste of the Christian way of life. He arrived after the family returned from the cathedral and shared their lunch of goose, Purna's best bird, and other traditional fare. He had been accepted into Anu's family – to Purna he was 'Captain' and to Kanchan, 'Romesh', in her Bengali accent. But they still worried about Anu's role in a Hindu household, should the two marry. There was no talk of marriage yet but they did not have long to wait.

In January, Gyan announced that his parents had arranged his marriage with a girl from the Punjab. He was to be married on the 15th of June.

The news motivated Ramesh into proposing to Anu. When he picked up the courage to ask for Anu's hand, Purna roared, 'Captain, have you ever faced a canon?' Ramesh's perplexed reply of 'No' completely missed the subtle implication that a mixed marriage could mean war, within the marriage or without. Ramesh assured the old man that Anu was under no pressure to convert to Hinduism. By the same token, Ramesh had no intention of changing his religion. Any future children would be raised with an appreciation of both religions and could make their choice when they were old enough. He also promised that, whenever possible, Anu would spend Christmas with her family in Allahabad. Purna decided to reserve his answer until he was sure Anu would be accepted by her Hindu in-laws. Ramesh asked his father to write to Purna, welcoming Anu into his family.

It was heartening for Purna and Kanchan to receive a letter from Lakshmi Dutt Vasisht expressing joy at his son's choice of mate. As thanksgiving to the gods, Lakshmi requested that an offering be made to the poor at a Hindu temple. The Sarkars had reservations about involvement in a Hindu rite, so Ramesh suggested an alternative. Why not make the offering, not at a Christian church nor at a Ḥindu temple, but at a Sikh gurdwara? The family complied with Lakshmi Dutt's request, Purna gave his blessing to the union and the couple got engaged. Ramesh placed a ring with three diamonds and sixteen rubies on Anu's finger. She gave her fiancé a signet ring engraved with the Ordnance crest. They planned to marry before the very hot summer or the very wet monsoon.

But national events overtook personal plans. On January 30, 1948 as Anu and her fiancé chatted on the chabutra, Purna hurried back from his evening stroll, taking a short-cut through the grounds of The Leader press. He rushed up to the couple.

'Captain!' he cried, 'Run! Mahatma Gandhi has been shot dead – they think by a Muslim. There is going to be mayhem on the streets!'

Ramesh leapt onto his motorbike and rode off, reaching Cheoki just as violent rioting took over the streets. It slowly emerged that Gandhi had been shot, not by a Muslim, but by a fellow-Hindu, incensed at the Mahatma's appeasement of Muslims. The country, barely recovered from the horrors of partition, was plunged into black despair at the loss of 'The Father of the Nation'.

After Gandhi, affectionately known as 'Bapu' (father), was cremated in Delhi, his ashes were brought to Allahabad, for immersion in the holy Sangam. A special train, painted white for mourning and draped with marigold garlands, carried his ashes from Delhi. In the central carriage, a raised dais bore the large copper urn of ashes. His closest disciples squatted around the urn, repeatedly chanting the Hindu dirge, 'Raghu pati raghav raja ram, patit a pavan sita ram...' – loosely translated as, 'O Lord God Almighty, have mercy on the fallen.'

At Allahabad railway station, the urn was removed from the train and placed on a gun-carriage. A military escort accompanied it through the city to the confluence of the holy rivers.

As All Saints Cathedral was close to the railway station, Anu waited with the choir, all dressed in white. When the cortege passed the gates, Anu was amazed to see Ramesh on the gun-carriage, beside the urn. As Liaison Officer between the military and civil authorities he was entrusted with overseeing the immersion of the ashes. The choir began to sing Gandhi's favourite Christian hymn, 'Lead Kindly Light'. Through their tears, they sang Cardinal Newman's well-known words until the procession was out of sight.

30
A VERY CIVIL MARRIAGE

After the period of national mourning was over, life regained some degree of normality. Anu and Ramesh resumed their wedding plans. The date they agreed on was the 15th of July. It was right in the middle of the monsoons but Ramesh's leave had been cancelled enough times and who knew what would happen next, with the country still struggling to get on its feet?

Anu resigned from her job at Hamidia Girls School and Kanchan set about organizing her daughter's wedding. The bride was to wear a white and gold silk sari. Her court shoes, from Mr Fookson's studio, would have the highest heels she could manage. At 4'10" Anu needed all the help she could get – her groom was 6'tall. Her ensemble was to be complemented by her mother's ruby and pearl suite. The famous Burmese rubies were acquired when Kanchan's sister lived in Burma. Ghanshyam Das, the family jeweller, set them in a Victorian style necklace and earrings. The necklace doubled as a tiara.

A few weeks before the wedding, a request for Anu's measurements arrived from Delhi – it seemed her wedding clothes would be supplied by her in-laws-to-be. Likewise, according to Hindu tradition, Ramesh's wedding outfit was to be provided by his future in-laws. Anu was dismayed but her father pointed out that this was only the first of many changes she would encounter as a

Christian in a Hindu household so she had better get used to it. Kanchan was dispatched to the fancy shops in Civil Lines to buy the groom's wedding clothes. She returned with a white silk dhoti and gold-edged stole and a silk kurta with gold and diamond buttons. She also bought a watch and gold cuff-links for Ramesh and prescribed outfits for his family members.

A party of nine baratis – groom's guests – travelled from Delhi for the wedding. Lakshmi Dutt was accompanied by his two younger sons, Munish and Raj, and six male friends including Mr Mullick, an eminent lawyer respectfully known as 'Mullick Sahib'. Purna, with Stan Boucher's help, rented a house in Chatham Lines for them and staffed it with cleaner and sweeper. He contracted Jagati & Sons, who ran the University canteen, to provide meals for the baratis. The Sarkar's neighbour, Zunnurain, was now Deputy Collector. Despite still having feelings for Anu, he generously offered the use of his chauffeur-driven car to facilitate her future in-laws.

On the morning of the wedding, Stan Boucher arrived at Kanchan Villa to deliver Anu's wedding ensemble and collect the clothes Ramesh was to wear. When Anu opened the case, her eyes welled up with tears. Despite sending her measurements to Delhi, the choli was far too big. The lavish yellow and gold sari was to be worn over a yellow slip embroidered with purple flowers. The outsized gold bangles slid off her slim wrists and the embroidered shoes were more suited to large Punjabi feet than Anu's dainty Bengali ones.

171

She was beginning to notice the subtler disparities in the two cultures.

Desperately searching for a match for her wedding sari, Anu found a gold brocade choli and yellow slip in her trousseau. She wore her in-law's gem encrusted necklace and earrings, but her own smaller gold bangles. Kanchan's Victorian tiara held her sari in place, over her covered head.

Being a mixed-marriage, the ceremony was a civil one. Given Purna's court connections, the Commissioner of Marriages agreed to perform the ceremony at Kanchan Villa. The family's right-hand man, Prashad, and Anu's sisters decorated the drawing room with flowers and streamers. There was a table and chair for the Commissioner, opposite whom the couple sat, on a sofa draped with garlands of red roses. Rows of chairs were placed on either side for the guests. Zunnurain quietly settled into a back row.

Ramesh wore the white silk outfit bought by Kanchan. She, too, had misread his measurements. The kurta was too short and the gossamer-fine silk allowed his underwear to show through. He spent the ceremony tugging at his kurta, in an attempt to cover his hips. Anu's throat went dry when the Commissioner asked her to 'profess no religion'. Her groom had already taken the oath. Anu whispered that she was Christian. The Commissioner explained that this was an important clause in the Special Marriage Act of 1876 – she had to state she 'professed no religion'. Anu felt hypocritical denying her god for the sake of her marriage.

The couple exchanged rings and the ceremony was over. Purna saw the Commissioner to his official car and guests crowded round to congratulate the couple. When the baratis came forward, Anu was instructed by her husband to touch the feet of her father-in-law as a gesture of respect. For the second time that day, she was reminded of the difference in cultures. Like a dutiful Hindu bride, she bent down and touched Laxmi Dutt's feet. When her own parents approached the couple, Anu wanted to cling to them and seek assurance that she was doing the right thing. Instead, she solemnly bent her head to receive their blessing.

Regaining her composure, Anu prepared to leave for the reception – but some folk had other ideas. With Sunny and Purnima no longer living at home, Purna had rented part of the house to a Bengali family. Now, the mother, Champa, insisted on standing in for the bride's Hindu mother-in-law. After blowing a conch shell, she chanted long prayers and then applied sindoor to indicate that Anu was now a married woman. She dipped a match-stick in oil, sprinkled the red powder on it and drew a line in Anu's hair parting with it. Unfortunately, the oil ran in a red trickle down Anu's forehead. When she wiped it away, she was left with a red forehead. But help was at hand. Her college friend, Bulbul Dey, cleaned and made up the bride's face again, covering the stubborn smudge on her forehead with a gold tikka from Anu's jewellery box.

'Now you look like a true Hindu bride,' she grinned at her friend.

Anu's lack of control over her appearance was evident from the wedding photo, taken by 'official photographer', Stan Boucher – she looked sombre and slightly detached beside her beaming new husband.

After the ceremony, Ramesh changed into his army uniform for the wedding reception in Barnett's Hotel, in civil Lines. The couple travelled in the bridal car with his father and brothers. By the time they arrived at the hotel, the heavens had opened in a fantastic display of monsoon rage. Guests, many from the army and law courts, were soaked in the dash from transport to hotel.

The wedding cake was multi-tiered, decorated with silver horse-shoes. On the topmost tier, two cupids held aloft the regimental crest of the Royal Ordnance Corps.

Ramesh mingled with his brother officers, leaving Anu alone on the bridal settee. Bulbul Dey approached the dais and sat beside her friend.

'Anu, this is what you wanted,' she said, taking the bride's cold hand in hers, 'remember, in Hindu culture when parents are present, men maintain a distance from their wives.'

Stan, seeing the bride alone on the dais, reminded Ramesh that he had not married a Hindu girl and should stay by her side through the evening.

The reception was followed by dinner for 'Nearest and Dearest' – a term favoured by Indian Christians – and catered by Jagati & Sons, in a shamianah at Kanchan Villa. There were two menus – vegetarian for the Hindu 'baratis' and non-vegetarian for the Sarkars' Christian friends. All the guests enjoyed wedding cake and a range of sweetmeats after the meal.

Before he left, Anu's new father-in-law handed Ramesh a silver filigree pillbox, for yet another little ceremony. The groom dipped his wedding ring in the red sindoor powder and rolled it along the parting in Anu's hair. This was followed by more feet-touching and a flurry of blessings. She was now a fully-fledged Hindu wife.

After the guests had departed, Ramesh decided to show off his new bride to his fellow officers in Cheoki, who had missed the wedding. Accompanied by Stan, the couple was driven in the bridal car, through deserted streets and relentless rain. At the army base, Anu was led from house to house, congratulated and toasted several times with various spirits, until Stan called a halt. When the car finally brought Anu back to Lukergunj, half the night was gone and it had never stopped raining. In bed, reflecting on the unremitting downpour, Anu wondered if it was significant that the sun had not shone on the bride at all. It was a thought that would come to mind many times in the future.

The next morning Purna gently shook his eldest daughter awake. Seeing the red smudge in the parting of her hair, his eyes misted over.

'You don't look any different to my little Pully of yesterday,' he whispered, 'except for the sindoor in your hair.'

Anu's trousseau had been lovingly packed in a black trunk by Kanchan, the jewellery boxes nestling amongst the clothes. In another trunk, she packed the traditional Hindu presents for Anu's in-laws.

Soon her new husband and baratis arrived to escort the bride to Delhi. Kanchan and her daughters huddled together and sobbed until Anu tore herself away. Purna, desperate to grasp every last minute with his beloved daughter, took Holly along to the railway station.

The bridal party boarded several reserved carriages. Purna was bewildered at this arrangement – Anu was the only woman in the party but the newly weds did not have a carriage to themselves.

The guard blew his whistle and the train slowly chugged out of the station. Purna and Holly ran along the platform, blowing kisses to the tearful Anu. When they reached the end of the platform and Anu's waving handkerchief became a tiny white speck, an emotional Purna turned to Holly and said, 'Our shepherd has left us.'